PROFILES IN
WORLD HISTORY

Significant Events and the People
Who Shaped Them

Volume 3: *The Crusades to Building Empires in the Americas, 1095-1500*

Crusades and Mongol Expansion
Saladin, Genghis Khan, Innocent III, Alexius V
Religion and Reason in the Middle Ages
Averroës, Maimonides, Thomas Aquinas
Beginning of Constitutional Government in England
Thomas Becket, King John
Muslim Influences on Empires in West Africa
Al-Bakri, Sundiata, Mansa Musa
Exploring the East
Marco Polo, William of Rubrouck, Ibn Battutah
Building Empires in Europe and Asia
Timur Lenk, Mehmed II, Ivan the Great, Babur
Building Empires in the Americas
Topa Inca Yupanqui, Moctezuma I

Volume 4: *The Age of Discovery to In 1400-1830*

Beginnings of the Age of Discovery
Cheng Ho, Vasco da Gama, Jacques Cartier
Religious Reform
Desiderius Erasmus, Guru Nanak, Ignatius of Loyola, Martin Luther
Revival of Science
Leonardo da Vinci, Tycho Brahe, Johannes Kepler
Revival of Literature
Francis Bacon, Miguel de Cervantes, William Shakespeare
Rise of Nationalism
Suleiman the Magnificent, Hideyoshi Toyotomi, Catherine the Great
Enlightenment
John Locke, Voltaire, Jean-Jacques Rousseau
Industrial Revolution
Charles Townshend, Richard Arkwright, James Watt

$\mathscr{P}$ROFILES IN
WORLD HISTORY

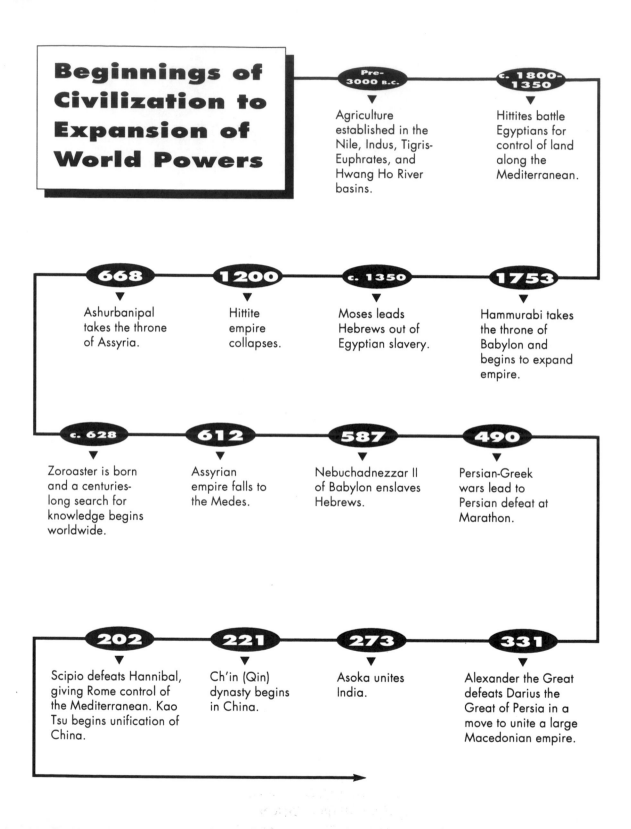

Beginnings of Civilization to Expansion of World Powers

Pre-3000 B.C.
Agriculture established in the Nile, Indus, Tigris-Euphrates, and Hwang Ho River basins.

c. 1800-1350
Hittites battle Egyptians for control of land along the Mediterranean.

668
Ashurbanipal takes the throne of Assyria.

1200
Hittite empire collapses.

c. 1350
Moses leads Hebrews out of Egyptian slavery.

1753
Hammurabi takes the throne of Babylon and begins to expand empire.

c. 628
Zoroaster is born and a centuries-long search for knowledge begins worldwide.

612
Assyrian empire falls to the Medes.

587
Nebuchadnezzar II of Babylon enslaves Hebrews.

490
Persian-Greek wars lead to Persian defeat at Marathon.

202
Scipio defeats Hannibal, giving Rome control of the Mediterranean. Kao Tsu begins unification of China.

221
Ch'in (Qin) dynasty begins in China.

273
Asoka unites India.

331
Alexander the Great defeats Darius the Great of Persia in a move to unite a large Macedonian empire.

PROFILES IN WORLD HISTORY

Significant Events and the People
Who Shaped Them

Beginnings of Civilization to
Expansion of World Powers

JOYCE MOSS
and
GEORGE WILSON

AN INT͏̮̮̮MPANY

PROFILES IN WORLD HISTORY
Significant Events and the People Who Shaped Them

VOLUME 1: BEGINNINGS OF CIVILIZATION TO EXPANSION OF WORLD POWERS

Joyce Moss and George Wilson

Staff

Carol DeKane Nagel, *U•X•L Developmental Editor*
Julie L. Carnagie, *U•X•L Assistant Editor*
Thomas L. Romig, *U•X•L Publisher*

Shanna P. Heilveil, *Production Assistant*
Evi Seoud, *Assistant Production Manager*
Mary Beth Trimper, *Production Director*

Barbara A. Wallace, *Permissions Associate (Pictures)*

Mary Krzewinski, *Cover and Page Designer*
Cynthia Baldwin, *Art Director*

The Graphix Group, *Typesetting*

∞™ This book is printed on acid-free paper that meets the minimum requirements of American National Standard for Information Sciences—Permanence Paper for Printed Library Materials, ANSI Z39.48-1984.

ISBN 0-7876-0464-X (Set)
ISBN 0-7876-0465-8 (v. 1)   ISBN 0-7876-0469-0 (v. 5)
ISBN 0-7876-0466-6 (v. 2)   ISBN 0-7876-0470-4 (v. 6)
ISBN 0-7876-0467-4 (v. 3)   ISBN 0-7876-0471-2 (v. 7)
ISBN 0-7876-0468-2 (v. 4)   ISBN 0-7876-0472-0 (v. 8)

Printed in the United States of America

I(T)P™ U·X·L is an imprint of Gale Research,
an International Thomson Publishing Company.
ITP logo is a trademark under license.

Contents

Beginnings of Civilization 1

Struggle for Control of the Middle East 42

Rise of Eastern Philosophies and Religions 78

Rise of Western Philosophies 108

Expansion of Macedonia 144

Expansion of World Powers 170

Reader's Guide

Profiles in World History: Significant Events and the People Who Shaped Them presents the life stories of more than 175 individuals who have played key roles in world history. The biographies are clustered around 50 broad events, ranging from the Rise of Eastern Religions and Philosophies to the Expansion of World Powers, from Industrial Revolution to Winning African Independence. Each biography—complete in itself—contributes a singular outlook regarding an event; when taken as cluster, the biographies provide a variety of views and experiences, thereby offering a broad perspective on events that shaped the world.

Those whose stories are told in *Profiles in World History* meet one or more of the following criteria. The individuals:

- Represent viewpoints or groups involved in a major world event
- Directly affected the outcome of the event
- Exemplify a role played by common citizens in that event

Format

Profiles in World History volumes are arranged by chapter. Each chapter focuses on one particular event and opens with an overview and detailed time line of the event that places it in historical context. Following are biographical profiles of two to five diverse individuals who played active roles in the event.

Each biographical profile is divided into four sections:

- **Personal Background** provides details that predate and anticipate the individual's involvement in the event

- **Participation** describes the role played by the individual in the event and its impact on his or her life

- **Aftermath** discusses effects of the individual's actions and subsequent relevant events in the person's life

- **For More Information** provides sources for further reading on the individual

Additionally, sidebars containing interesting details about the events and individuals profiled are interspersed throughout the text.

Additional Features

Portraits, illustrations, and maps as well as excerpts from primary source materials are included in *Profiles in World History* to help bring history to life. Sources of all quoted material are cited parenthetically within the text, and complete bibliographic information is listed at the end of each biography. A full bibliography of scholarly sources consulted in preparing each volume appears in each book's back matter.

Cross references are made in the entries, directing readers to other entries within the volume that are connected in some way to the person under scrutiny. Additionally, each volume ends with a subject index, while Volume 8 concludes with a cumulative subject index, providing easy access to the people and events mentioned throughout *Profiles in World History*.

Comments and Suggestions

We welcome your comments on this work as well as your suggestions for individuals to be featured in future editions of *Profiles in World History*. Please write: Editors, *Profiles in World History*, U·X·L, 835 Penobscot Bldg., Detroit, Michigan 48226-4094; fax to 313-961-6348; or call toll-free: 1-800-877-4253.

Acknowledgments

The editors would like to thank the many people involved in the preparation of *Profiles in World History*.

For guidance in the choice of events and personalities, we are grateful to Ross Dunn, Professor of History at the University of California at San Diego, and David Smith, Professor of History at California Polytechnic University at Pomona. We're thankful to Professor Smith for his careful review of the entire series and his guidance toward key sources of information about personalities and events.

We deeply appreciate the writers who compiled data and contributed to the biographies: Diane Ahrens, Bill Boll, Qucsiyah Ali Chavez, Charity-Jean Conklin, Mario Cutajar, Craig Hinkel, Hillary Manning, Lawrence Orr, Phillip T. Slattery, Colin Wells, and Susan Yun. We'd especially like to thank Jamie Mohn and Cheryl Steets for their careful attention to the manuscript.

Thanks also to the copy editors and proofreaders, Sonia Benson, Barbara C. Bigelow, Betz Des Chenes, Robert Griffin, Rob Nagel, and Paulette Petrimoulx, for their careful attention to style and detail. Special thanks to Margaret M. Johnson, Judith Kass, and John F. Petruccione for researching the illustrations and maps.

And, finally, thanks to Carol Nagel of U·X·L for overseeing the production of the series.

Picture Credits

The photographs and illustrations appearing in *Profiles in World History: Significant Events and the People Who Shaped Them,* Volume 1: *Beginnings of Civilization to Expansion of World Powers* were received from the following sources:

On the cover: **The Bettmann Archive:** Aristotle; Hatshepsut; Siddhartha Gautama.

Archive Photos: pp. 4, 8, 10, 25, 39, 66, 74, 81, 125, 192; **Archive Photos/Popperfoto:** p. 103; **The Bettmann Archive:** pp. 18, 20, 63, 64, 73, 94, 106, 116, 121, 137, 139, 141, 147, 149, 154, 160, 172, 187, 189, 200; **The Granger Collection:** pp. 15, 47, 55, 71, 76, 83, 98, 175; **Joseph Needham,** *The Great Titration*, **Allen & Unwin:** p. 7; **Library of Congress:** pp. 17, 21, 29, 37, 49, 57, 58, 133, 181; **Outlook Films Ltd.:** p. 197; **Reuters/Bettmann:** p. 165; **Springer/Bettmann Film Archive:** p. 151; **UPI/Bettmann:** pp. 90, 178.

Beginnings of Civilization

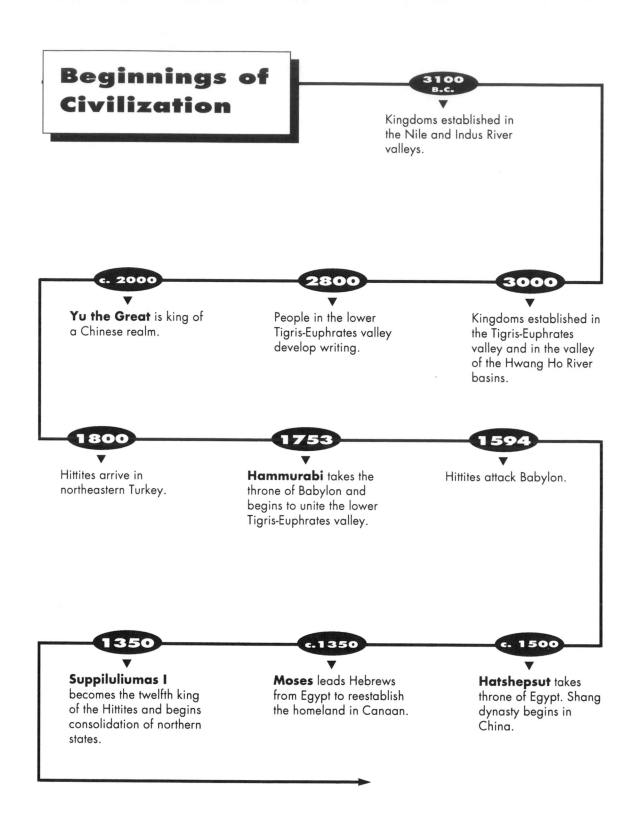

3100 B.C.
Kingdoms established in the Nile and Indus River valleys.

3000
Kingdoms established in the Tigris-Euphrates valley and in the valley of the Hwang Ho River basins.

2800
People in the lower Tigris-Euphrates valley develop writing.

c. 2000
Yu the Great is king of a Chinese realm.

1800
Hittites arrive in northeastern Turkey.

1753
Hammurabi takes the throne of Babylon and begins to unite the lower Tigris-Euphrates valley.

1594
Hittites attack Babylon.

c. 1500
Hatshepsut takes throne of Egypt. Shang dynasty begins in China.

c. 1350
Moses leads Hebrews from Egypt to reestablish the homeland in Canaan.

1350
Suppiluliumas I becomes the twelfth king of the Hittites and begins consolidation of northern states.

BEGINNINGS
OF
CIVILIZATION

More than five thousand years ago, people who had once obtained their food by hunting animals and gathering plants discovered how to farm. By 3000 B.C. farmers had settled in the great river valleys of the Middle East and Asia—along the Nile River in Egypt, in the middle land (Mesopotamia) between the Tigris and Euphrates Rivers (in what is now Iraq), in the Indus Valley of India, and along the Yellow River and its tributaries in China.

Soon the farmers began to live together in villages to protect themselves from the tribes of hunters around them. The villagers then found that only part of their time was needed to produce enough food. These farming communities evolved to also include craftspeople, who specialized in making needed tools and creating products for trade.

There were, however, many peoples who kept to the old nomadic hunting and gathering lifestyle. They quickly discovered the wealth of the villagers, and added raiding to their methods of obtaining food and other necessities. Villagers countered these raids by building stout walls around their communities. In time, these walled communities became thriving cities in which nobility, businesspeople, and craftspeople lived and worked. These specialists lived inside the walls, while farmers lived and tended

▲ A bas relief of men bearing tribute and gifts, including monkeys, for the king, from Ashurbanipal's palace at Calah. Powerful kings demanded tribute payments from the smaller cities around them.

fields within sight of the fortifications. Soon standing armies were needed to protect the lands of the farmers, the power of the kings, and the wealth of the merchants.

Writing. Business also brought a need for better communication. As early as 2800 B.C., city dwellers began to develop ways of writing and keeping records. Early scribes, or record-keepers, wrote on clay tablets or bones or papyrus, a kind of paper made from grass. They wrote in hieroglyphics, or forms of picture writing, and then in a script of triangular marks called cuneiform. It is mostly from these records, stored in the earliest libraries, that we know the stories of these ancient civilizations. About one thousand years later, in the eighteenth century B.C., the Babylonian king **Hammurabi** set down his code. Though he was not the first lawgiver, he was the most famous: he left his laws inscribed in stone.

Kings and kingdoms. Wealth also encouraged power. Each major city became an independent state controlled by a king, who often claimed to be assigned the job by a god, or to be himself a god. The more powerful kings began to demand tribute, or payments, from the smaller cities around them, and then sought control of agriculture and trade in larger areas. Sargon the Great unified the cities of the lower Tigris and Euphrates Rivers from his capital city, Ur. Pharaohs took control of the whole Nile River valley from bases such as Thebes and Memphis. In China, too, the civilized peoples decided very early that for their protection it was better to unite under a single ruler.

The Middle East, however, was a melting pot into which new peoples poured and established themselves in new kingdoms: Ur, on a channel of the Euphrates, gave way to Babylon some distance up the river. In the north, Assyrian people built a powerful empire with its capital at Nineveh. Some time before 1800 B.C., another people from the north, the Hittites, moved into what is now northeastern Turkey. There in the rocky foothills where the Taurus Mountains join the Caucasus Mountains, they built cities such as Hattusa and established the empire of Hatti. Assyria, Babylonia, and Hatti were but a few of the kingdoms that were frequently at war for control of the area and, most importantly, for trade.

Some distance away, Egypt, under a single ruler (the pharaoh), was able to develop its trade and expand its influence across the Sinai Desert and along the coast of the Mediterranean

▲ Hebrews in bondage in Egypt. Though never a ruling power in the Middle East, the Hebrews nonetheless were a constant obstacle to rulers who wanted to control the Mediterranean coastal area. Hebrew lands were often overrun by invaders, who would enslave the people.

Sea, sometimes as far as Syria. Thus Egypt became a major player in the power struggles of the Middle East.

China. While many of the records of the Middle East and Egypt remain, the early records of China were either destroyed or remain hidden. Only in the 1950s did the search for evidence of Chinese ancient history begin. So far, pottery, statuary, and writing—mostly on the bones of deer or the shells of turtles—are the only clues beyond oral histories that tell us about Chinese beginnings. One of the legends describes a great humanitarian and engineer who became king of China through his service to the kingdom. This king, **Yu the Great,** may or may not be a real person, but his story illustrates the Chinese dedication to selecting a king for his goodness and wisdom.

Hebrews. The people of Judah and Israel, known as the Hebrews, were never a ruling power in the Middle East, but they were a constant obstacle to rulers who wanted to control the Mediterranean coastal area. Hebrew lands, therefore, were frequently overrun by invaders, who carried the Hebrews off to become slaves in Babylon or Egypt. They came to prefer bondage in Egypt over bondage in Babylon. But one time, as slaves in Egypt, the Hebrews did rise up against the pharaoh under one of the greatest ancient heroes, **Moses.** Moses himself is something of a mystery. No mention of him is found in any Egyptian literature; the only record comes from the Bible.

Women. Women in early history were little more than slaves, although women of the royal houses received special treatment. Ankhesenamen briefly ruled Egypt after the death of her husband, Tutankhamen, commonly known as King Tut. **Hatshepsut** was another Egyptian woman who rose to kingship. She ruled for twenty years by having the priests proclaim that the gods had made her king and by playing that role in male costume throughout her reign. Though these women rose to power in spite of male domination, the treatment women received at the hands of Hittite king **Suppiluliumas I** is more indicative of women's standing in ancient societies: he cemented his agreements with surrounding nations by giving his sister and daughter to other rulers to add to their harems.

Yu the Great

c. 2020-c. 1970 B.C.

Personal Background

A cloud of mystery. A great cloud hangs over the ancient history of the Chinese people. Names, dates, and actual events remain a mystery, even though the nation's people have had a written language for thousands of years. Much of the writing was not saved, and history was passed on solely by word of mouth until about 500 B.C., when Chinese philosopher and educator Confucius set out to record the history, beliefs, and basic ideas of Chinese society in nine books. Later, an emperor who wanted to make his own rule the most important in Chinese history ordered these books destroyed. Scholars struggled to rewrite the important books of Confucius after the emperor's death, but it is difficult to judge how accurately they preserved the author's original text.

Digging up the past. In the 1920s Chinese scholars began to study the ruins of their ancient societies. But their work was stopped when the Japanese threatened China and claimed rule over much of the land. Still, the diggings that were completed showed that great empires existed more than four thousand years ago. It has been determined that cities and villages lined the river valleys of northeastern China during that time.

Clues to how the ancient Chinese people lived have been uncovered in the "oracle bones," deer bones said to bear mes-

▲ **Yu the Great leaving home to tame the raging floodwaters.**

Event: Developing an agricultural society in China.

Role: Yu is believed by some to be a mythical character of ancient China who saved his nation from destruction by taming raging floodwaters that flowed out of the country's mountains, threatening farmlands. However, recent efforts by the Chinese to uncover ancient ruins suggest that Yu was a real person—the first of a family of rulers who governed a Chinese society until about 1766 B.C.

▲ **Entrance of the Hwang Ho, or Yellow River, one of the great rivers that roar through the narrow canyons of the China mountains.**

sages to and from the dead. For centuries the Chinese people have believed that their ancestors possess the power to look after them. Ancient peoples of the Shang era (1766-1122 B.C.) communicated with their deceased loved ones by writing questions to them on the bones of deer or on tortoise shells. These "oracle bones" cracked when they were heated, and priests read the ancestors' answers from the cracks. But because China was closed for many years to foreigners, these and other writings were not translated into different languages. Nevertheless such sources offer some insight into a well-organized society that was run by some of the greatest rulers in history.

The land of Yu. In the north of China mountains rise in all directions, reaching heights of more than ten thousand feet and separating the great river basins from the high Mongolian plateau. Great rivers roar through narrow canyons toward the Pacific Ocean. One such river, the Hwang Ho (also spelled Huang He and known as Yellow River), flows first east from the highest mountains, then turns sharply south toward the mountain bases, then swings in a sharp arc to flow east again through a broad plain toward the Yellow Sea.

Some four thousand years ago, reigning emperors made their city homes at the site where the Hwang Ho makes its last turn toward the sea. These emperors ruled over hundreds of villages of farmers, hunters, and herders. Herds of oxen, dogs, and sheep provided meat for the villagers. Although the people had not yet learned to use metal to make farm tools, the soil was rich and easy to work using wooden tools, so the empires prospered. More than enough millet (a type of grass) was grown to feed the people, and surplus quantities were traded. Fishermen worked the Hwang Ho, which was teeming with fish, to add to the food supply.

According to ancient Chinese legend, Yu was a farmer in his youth. He and his family lived much like the other peasant families in his village, one of many that had sprung up around the great rivers a few hundred years earlier. Theirs was a large society governed by lords who paid allegiance to the emperor and his priests. Although Yu's grandfather had once been emperor, Yu had no claim to the throne. At this time in Chinese history, landowners selected the best man in the society—regardless of his family history—to succeed a dying emperor.

In addition to tending the millet or rice on his farm, Yu is believed to have been an active hunter. His wife spun yarn and made clothing while caring for the family and their simple home. Pots for cooking, storing, and carrying, created by coiling clay in circles one on top of the other, made up most of the household wares.

Yu probably built his family's house, which was made of wood and constructed on a foundation of pounded soil. His knowledge of mathematics was extremely valuable in this task. He knew that boards fashioned into a triangle—with side lengths measured in multiples of 3, 4, and 5—could help him make the corners of his house square.

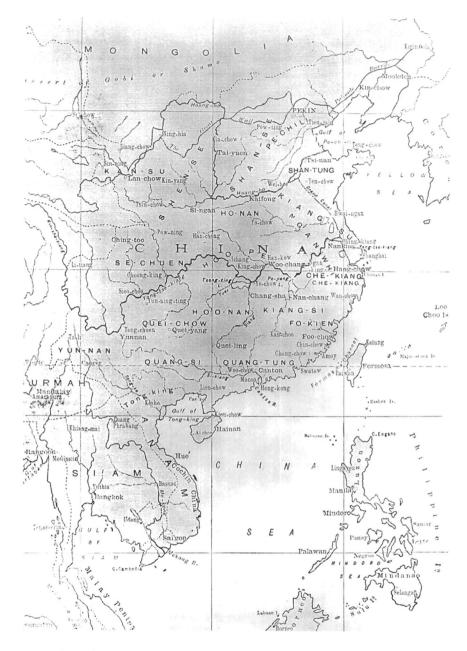

▲ In China the civilized peoples decided very early that for their protection it was better to unite under a single ruler.

The streams. Yu learned to use the surveying tools of his day, including special sighting tools, poles marked for measuring, and a plumb line. He knew how to measure greater distances with a string and could even record his measurements using the old Chinese system of bars. He was also able to read the shadow of a gnomon (something like the pointer in a sun dial) to tell the time of day and mark the seasons.

Floods. All this knowledge helped Yu manage his land and thrive as a successful farmer. Better than any other person in the village, Yu could direct the flow of water to irrigate his crops while avoiding the annual floods. These floods fed the soil with layers of silt, or rocky sediment, and destroyed crops and houses along the streambeds.

Participation: Taming the Floods

A terrible year. Chinese legend indicates that the floods were especially devastating one particular year around four millenia ago. All the rivers that flow into the Hwang Ho—the Tsu (also spelled Zu), Luliang, Jui (or Rui), Wei, and many smaller streams—overflowed their banks. Villagers perched on terraces above the streams; many lost their homes, their farms, even their lives to the raging waters.

Southward in what is now the Chinese province of Honan (also spelled Henan) lay the capital city of Yang-Hsia (or Yangxia), where the emperor lived. Concerned about the protection and well-being of his people, the emperor sought assistance in controlling the floodwaters and ensuring that similar damage could be avoided in the future.

Someone apparently remembered hearing about a peasant in a distant village who was said to have controlled the waters near his own village—a man called Yu. The emperor sent for Yu and begged him to help control the floods. Although he had a wife, children, and a farm of his own to worry about, Yu agreed to the larger task of helping his nation.

> ### The Role of the Gods in Ancient Chinese Life
>
> Like most of his neighbors, Yu sought guidance from the gods and from his ancestors. The chief god was Pan Ku (also spelled Ban Gu), the oldest of the mythical figures in the Chinese story of creation. There was also Sui Len, the god-man who discovered fire; Fu Hsi (or Fu Xi), who was said to have invented marriages and who looked after married couples; and Shin Hong, who is thought to have introduced farming to the world and understood the value of plants in curing ills.

Yu the engineer. The stories of Yu's intelligence and hero-
ism have been passed down by word of mouth for generations.
According to folklore, he gathered his tools, traveled to the capital
city, and began his work, using his knowledge of engineering to
block the annual floods. For thirteen years he oversaw work on
the nation's many rivers. Under his direction, the riverbeds were
deepened, the paths of dangerous streams were changed, and
dams were built to slow the water flow. In the end, Yu made
ancient China a safer place for the farmers and helped them to
improve their crops. China's cities had already been centers of
trade with cities of the Middle East; now the nation's abundant
crops and safe homes on the river terraces allowed Chinese trade
to grow.

Yu was so dedicated to his task that he spent all his time
working. Ancient legend tells us that he only ventured home
three times in thirteen years, and then only near enough to hear
his children cry. Never again, so the story goes, did he enter his
own house.

Aftermath

Emperor Yu. As the Chinese emperor grew older, the
search for an able, wise, and considerate successor began. Yu was
clearly the best choice to rule the land. When the old emperor
died, Yu became emperor of all China.

Yu was a popular, well-respected ruler who relied heavily on
the gods and his ancestors for advice on how to govern. During
his reign, he is said to have received the gifts of two charts: one
known as the Luo Shu came from a turtle who lived in the Luo
River; the other, He Thu, was given to him by a dragon horse who
lived in the Yellow River. Both charts helped guide his actions.

After Yu's death, the Hsia (also spelled Xia) people, as the
people of China were then called, abandoned their own tradition.
The lords did not search outside the royal family for a new
emperor but insisted that Yu's son assume the position of leadership in the kingdom. Thus began the first "dynasty," a period of

rule by a single family. The family of Yu ruled the land for more than three hundred years.

The end of the dynasty. In 1557 B.C., the Hsia dynasty came to an end when the Yu family emperor proved to be an evil tyrant. He was soon overthrown and replaced by a member of the Shang family, thus marking the start of another dynasty. This new dynasty is the first for which any real records have been uncovered. Although some students of ancient Chinese culture still question the very existence of Yu's Hsia dynasty, the legend of Yu the Great lives on.

For More Information

Fitzgerald, C. P. *China: A Short Cultural History.* New York: Frederick A. Praeger, 1954.

Ho Ping-Ti. *The Cradle of the East: An Enquiry into the Indigenous Origins of Techniques and Ideas of Neolithic and Early Historic China, 5000 B.C. to 1000 B.C.* Chicago: University of Chicago Press, 1975.

Li Chi. *The Formation of the Chinese People.* Cambridge, Massachusetts: Harvard University Press, 1928.

Needham, Joseph. *Clerks and Craftsmen in China and the West.* Cambridge, England: Cambridge University Press, 1970.

Ronan, Colin A. *The Shorter Science and Civilization in China.* 3 vols. Cambridge, England: Cambridge University Press, 1988.

Hammurabi

c. 1815-1750 B.C.

Personal Background

A prince. Clay tablets and other documents provide some information about the ancient city of Babylon as far back as 1800 B.C. By studying the centuries-old documents, scholars have been able to piece together the history of the city and speculate on what life might have been like for Hammurabi, the son of King Sinmuballit of Babylon, as a young prince.

Mesopotamia. The name Mesopotamia, which means "the land between the rivers," refers to the region of southwest Asia that lies between the Tigris and Euphrates Rivers. Around the eighteenth century B.C., Babylon was just one of several kingdoms in those fertile river valleys, located in what is now the republic of Iraq. Farming communities had grown into towns along the lengths of the rivers, and expansion continued as the people learned more about irrigation. All along the lower regions of the two rivers, canals and ditches carried water to irrigate crops as far as four miles away.

The Tigris and the Euphrates also provided trade routes to the south, west, and east. As more and more small towns were transformed into rich trade centers, a system of royal rule began to emerge. Each king sought to control as much of the area around his city as possible. Thus Elam, Amur, Nineveh, Larsa, Eshnunna, and other cities of the Middle East became separate

▲ **Hammurabi**

Event: Building the Babylonian empire.

Role: Taking rule as the sixth king of Babylon, Hammurabi led this city-state to dominate the lower regions of the Tigris and Euphrates River valleys. He established firm control by expanding a system of rigid laws to control the daily lives of his subjects.

kingdoms. In some cases, the larger, more powerful city-states exerted political pressure on neighboring states, forcing them to pay tribute, or a sort of ransom, in order to maintain their independence. Such was the situation in the time of Sinmuballit's reign. Babylon was a separate country but paid tribute to the king of Elam, a dominant nation nearby.

The childhood of a prince. Sinmuballit and his family lived in a walled palace within the fortified city of Babylon. Archaeologists have unearthed the remains of a similar palace belonging to the king of another river state. Aside from the monarch's living quarters, the palace and its grounds—spread out over six acres—comprised a city within a city from which the affairs of government and commerce were controlled. Various government agents also lived there, and politicians oversaw all the nation's trade from business offices within the palace.

Where Was Babylon?

The land near the Tigris and Euphrates Rivers has changed greatly over time. At one point, the Persian Gulf extended far north of its present boundary, and the two rivers ran separate courses, entering the gulf at different places. Ancient Babylon was on the banks of the Euphrates River, but its location may have changed as the river's course shifted. The site of the Babylonian capital has been excavated, or uncovered, by archaeologists. Situated around a central temple called a ziggurat, the city may have been founded as long as fifty-five hundred years ago.

As a young prince, Hammurabi probably learned a great deal about the nations of the Middle East. He was taught to read the Akkadian language used in the city and is thought to have studied the general living conditions of the people of the valley states. Scholars also suspect that the prince practiced archery and gained experience in the use of other tools of war. When he grew older, he may have accompanied his father on raids by the forces of Babylon and Elam against other nations.

King of Babylon. After his father's death, Hammurabi became the king of Babylon. The nation was still paying tribute to the king of Elam, at this time Kudur Mabuk, but Elam was soon overshadowed by another growing city-state, Larsa, governed by King Rim Sin. Ancient records indicate that there was no supreme ruler in the rivers area at this point in the eighteenth century B.C. Hammurabi controlled nearly the same number of

▲ Remains of Babylon's city walls; it is believed the city was founded
fifty-five hundred years ago.

lesser kings as did Rim Sin of Larsa and Ibal-pi-El of the kingdom
of Eshnunna. Amut-pi-El of Quatnum, located to the northeast in
Syria, and Yarim-Lim of Yamkhad, far in the north, were other
influential leaders of the time. It was not long, however, before
Hammurabi led his army to defeat Rim Sin and began to shape
Babylon into the most powerful nation in the Persian Gulf's delta
area.

Builder. After achieving peace and gaining complete independence for Babylon, Hammurabi mounted a campaign to
restore the city and thus bring his empire to its greatest power.
He built new canals to increase the quality and quantity of avail-

▲ Hammurabi presiding over a trial; in order to enforce his code of laws fairly, Hammurabi had to change the justice system in Babylon.

able farmland and produce more goods for trade. Large granaries were erected to store vast amounts of barley, the nation's main crop and trade product. And as the city grew in population and wealth, the king had its walls expanded. He also set out to control more land in the valley until his empire reached as far north as the present-day city of Baghdad and as far south as the ancient city of Ur on the Persian Gulf.

Model state. With peace and prosperity ensured, Hammurabi set up a model government for the city of Babylon. Declaring himself "the king of righteousness," he strove "to make justice visible in the land, to destroy the wicked person and the evil-doer, that the strong might not injure the weak." In order to accomplish this, he shaped a set of laws regulating almost all aspects of ordinary citizens' lives; in this way, he wrote, he could "set right the orphan and widow ... and wronged person" (Saggs 1965, p. 137). The laws of Babylon are believed to be the most complete of any of the ancient codes that have been discovered.

Participation:
The Code of Hammurabi

Hammurabi's code of laws—said to be inspired by the sun god Shumash—was carved into a large black stone more than seven feet tall. The laws were laid out in columns on both sides of the stone and included 280 sections describing legal procedures, property rights, loans, deposits, debts, family rights, women's rights, the treatment of the poor, and even schedules of payments for services. Each law was accompanied by an explanation of the penalty for failing to uphold it.

In order to enforce his code of laws fairly, Hammurabi had to change the justice system in Babylon. Religious leaders had served as judges for many years, but the king felt that they had become much too powerful. He soon replaced them with elders from the nation's "gentleman" class. New courts were established, and new judges were appointed for life terms. Hammurabi also organized separate departments of government similar to those that exist today in modern nations. Each department reported directly to him to ensure his supreme control.

Some of Hammurabi's Laws

If a gentleman's wife has had her husband killed on account of another man, they shall impale that woman on a stake.

If a son has struck his father, they shall cut off his hand.

If a man's ox is habitually given to goring, and the man's local authority has notified him that it is habitually given to goring, and he has not protected its horns nor restrained his ox, and that ox has gored a man of the "gentleman" class and caused his death, he shall pay half a mina of silver. If the man killed is a gentleman's slave, he shall pay one-third of a mina of silver.

If a man has come forward in a lawsuit for the witnessing of false things, and has not proved the thing that he said, if that lawsuit is a capital case, that man shall be put to death. (Saggs 1965, pp. 141-44)

▲ The Code of Hammurabi, which is said to have been inspired by the sun god Shumash.

Aftermath

Years after Hammurabi's rule, Babylon lost dominance and Elam again grew into a more powerful city-state. Babylon then faded into near disappearance for more than one thousand years. In the sixth century B.C., however, it was revived and brought into even greater grandeur by another famous king, Nebuchadnezzar II.

In 1901 the stele, or stone, upon which the Code of Hammurabi was written was found by French researchers in Susa, the main city of Elam. It had broken into three pieces. Because the laws were written in the Akkadian language, it was some time before anyone was able to translate them. The ancient stone was later repaired and is now stored in the Louvre, the famous French museum in Paris.

For More Information

Oates, Joan C. *Babylon*. London: Thames and Hudson, 1979.

Saggs, H. W. E. *Before Greece and Rome*. New Haven, Connecticut: Yale University Press, 1989.

Saggs, H. W. E. *Everyday Life in Babylonia and Assyria*. London: B. T. Batsford, 1965.

Wellard, James Howard. *Babylon*. New York: Saturday Review Press, 1972.

Hatshepsut

c. 1530-1482 B.C.

Personal Background

Traditions in ancient Egypt. Four thousand years ago, the country of Egypt was nothing more than a narrow strip of land through which the Nile River flowed northward to the Mediterranean Sea, with a rich delta at its mouth. The land was ruled by a line of kings who claimed to be direct descendants of one of the gods. Polygamy, or marriage to more than one person at the same time, was a common practice among Egyptian kings. When a king designated one of his wives to be his chief wife, the couple entered into a sacred marriage: that wife was united with the god who inhabited the king's body. A son born from such a marriage was destined to be the next king.

Thus it happened that King Thutmose I named Ahmose, said to be the most beautiful woman in the land, as his chief wife. According to legend, Amon-Re, the god of the Egyptian capital of Thebes, announced to the other gods that he was about to father a new king. Amon-Re turned himself into Thutmose I, and the god/king and his intended wife underwent a sacred ceremony. They later had a child, but this child was a girl, Hatshepsut (pronounced "hat **shep** soot").

Regent. Hatshepsut grew up in the palace at Thebes and married her half brother Thutmose II, who claimed the throne. But their marriage did not result in a male heir—Hatshepsut bore

▲ **Hatshepsut**

Event: Building trade between Egypt and other nations.

Role: During her reign as king of Egypt, Hatshepsut built great monuments as well as a fleet to sail the Red Sea to trade with the ancient nation of Punt.

two girls. Meanwhile, Thutmose II had fathered a son by one of his other wives. That son, Thutmose III, was widely considered to be heir to the throne. But his father died while he was still very young, and Hatshepsut was named regent, or ruler, until the boy reached adulthood. Hatshepsut had no thoughts of giving up the throne, however. Carefully, she tried to convince the Egyptians that she was the rightful ruler.

Propaganda and the throne. Across the river from Thebes, at Dier el Bahri, Hatshepsut built a great temple to the god Amon-Re. She had the temple painted with scenes of her parents' sacred marriage, her birth, and Amon's welcoming the baby girl, claiming, "A king are you, who shall wear the royal crowns in eternal possession of the throne" (Säve-Söderbergh, p. 56). The few existing sculptures of her often show a woman in man's clothing, wearing a king's crown from which straps hold a false beard, the common symbol of kings of Egypt.

> ## How a Woman Became King
>
> Hatshepsut was not the only woman to rule in ancient Egypt. There was a ruling queen around 2300 B.C. and one in 1900 B.C. Then, sometime around 1200 B.C., another queen, Tausert, called herself king.
>
> Hatshepsut was unique, however, in that in order to rule Egypt, she disguised herself as a man and arranged for the god Amon-Re to name her king.

Hatshepsut also had scribes write about her beauty and her godliness:

> Her Majesty became greater than all things, more beautiful to view than all things. Her form was that of a god, her character was that of a god. She acted in all things as a god would act.... [She is] Amon's glorious image, his living statue on earth. (Säve-Söderbergh, p. 57)

The propaganda worked. Hatshepsut was able to hold the throne even after Thutmose III had become an adult.

Monuments to Amon-Re. At the great temple to Amon-Re, Hatshepsut made another grand announcement. Far up the river lay the town of Aswan with its great quarries of fine stone. She would have two giant obelisks, or stone pillars, carved from the quarry, then moved by riverboat to Thebes to be raised in front of the temple of Amon-Re. Each great stone would stand more than 100 feet tall, be 6 feet across, and weigh nearly 350 tons. Deco-

▲ The temple of Hatshepsut at Luxor, Egypt, was built to honor the god
Amon-Re, Hatshepsut's "father."

rated with silver and gold, the temple would stand for centuries as
a monument to the god and his daughter. The raising of the
obelisks was a great task, one worthy of glory. Hatshepsut took
care to have written down all that was done.

Participation: The Excursion to Punt

Despite Hatshepsut's building of monuments to the gods,
there were those who still thought that Thutmose III was the
rightful king. Also, because she was a woman, Hatshepsut could
not lead the Egyptian army as a warrior-god/king was expected to
do. For these reasons she was not always popular, but she did
manage to expand Egyptian trade, farmland, and wealth. Perhaps
her greatest accomplishment was expanding trade with Punt.

Egyptians sailed far on the Nile River and Mediterranean Sea
to trade. They went all the way to Lebanon, for example, for the

The Raising of the Obelisks

Thousands of workers toiled under the hot sun and overseers' whips to carve and erect the great obelisks, stones similar to the Washington Monument in Washington, D.C.

First the stones were heated with bonfires and water was poured on them to make the surfaces crack. Since there were no metal tools, hundreds of workers used harder rocks to smooth the cracked surface. More workers used the hard rocks as hammers to separate the stones from their beds. Thousands of workers then jostled each great stone onto a sled and dragged it down a mud street to the shore of the river. There a great barge, two hundred feet long, awaited in dry dock. When a stone was slid into place, water was let in and the great barge floated. Ships manned by rows of oarsmen took the rocks downriver to Thebes.

Meanwhile, foundations were being built for the great obelisks, as well as a ramp with great holes filled with sand. The stones were dragged up the ramp until the heavier ends were high above the earth and supported by the sand. As workers dug out the sand, the tall stones began to slide upright into the foundations.

wood needed for shipbuilding. And during the reigns of earlier kings, they journeyed hundreds of miles to the fabled land of Punt in search of the perfumes incense and myrrh. Hatshepsut decided that her ships must travel there as well for these precious commodities. But there was no direct water route to Punt, which may have been on the horn of Africa, where Somalia now sits. One could begin the trip on the Nile and finish on the Red Sea, but there was no way to get by water from one waterway to the other. Between the two lay more than one hundred miles of rugged, rocky desert. The best path between the Nile and the Red Sea led along a dry wash, or a dry streambed, that began about thirty miles below the Egyptian capital at Thebes.

Hatshepsut sent an expedition to Punt. All of the voyagers participating in the trip carried twenty containers of water apiece as they crossed the desert to the Red Sea. There they built combination-powered ships (when the wind blew, sails provided the power; when the wind failed, oarsmen rowed) and set sail. After trading with the people of Punt, they returned by the same route. Though many trips to Punt had been taken under previous kings without much excitement, Hatshepsut made the most of it. Scenes describing the trip were constructed for Hatshepsut's temple.

Aftermath

Accomplishments. Hatshepsut ruled Egypt for twenty years. Though she did much to promote trade and industry and encouraged imaginative architecture throughout the land, she was still not well liked, particularly by those who thought her claim to the throne unjust. Indeed, her close friend Senenmut, builder of her temple, realized her unpopularity. He secretly made himself two tombs—one near Hatshepsut's temple, and another deep below the temple walls. He feared that hatred for Hatshepsut would result in the destruction of his visible grave. He was right.

Death. When Hatshepsut died, she was buried as she had planned—not in the graveyard for royal women but in the valley of the kings with the male rulers of the past. Finally, Thutmose III, the son of her half brother Thutmose II, took control of Egypt. It was 1483 B.C., and all the small kingdoms of Palestine and Syria were joining to shake the rule of Egypt. Thutmose led his armies on battles nearly every year of his reign to quiet this rebellion in the north. He proved to be the great war leader that Hatshepsut could not have been.

Thutmose III, however, could never forgive Hatshepsut for taking the throne he believed to be his. When she died, he ordered all statues of her destroyed and her name struck from all records. Even her deeds were assigned to others, Thutmose II or Thutmose III, so it would appear in history that Hatshepsut had never ruled Egypt, nor for that matter even existed.

> ## The Succession to the Throne of Egypt
>
> During Hatshepsut's twenty-year rule, the only wars in Egypt were for control of the northern border. She was thus able to concentrate on creating great buildings and improving business and trade. The kings before and after her were warriors, and they all carried the same name: Thutmose I, Thutmose II, Hatshepsut, then Thutmose III. Thutmose III fought a major war each year for sixteen years.

For More Information

Mertz, Barbara. *Red Land, Black Land: Daily Life in Ancient Egypt.* New York: Dodd, Mead & Company, 1978.

Murray, Margaret A. *The Splendor That Was Egypt.* New York: Hawthorn Books, 1963.

Säve-Söderbergh, Torgny. *Pharaohs and Mortals.* Translated from Swedish by Richard E. Oldenburg. London: Robert Hale, 1961.

Suppiluliumas I

c. 1400-c. 1335 B.C.

Personal Background

The Hittites. Little is known about the origin of the Hittite people, but they probably came from lands to the northeast of the Mediterranean Sea. Prior to 1800 B.C., they settled in the foothills of the Taurus and Caucasus Mountains in what is now Turkey. There, protected by the rugged rocks, the Hittites built the capital city of Hattusas. The city was destroyed by order of King Anittas of nearby Kussara around 1800 B.C., then rebuilt by the Hittites, but destroyed once more 350 years later. Hattusas was being resurrected for a third time when Suppiluliumas (pronounced "suh pil loo **lee** uh mas")began his rule as king of Hatti in the middle of the fourteenth century B.C. The city spanned six square miles and eventually housed five temples.

Early life. Suppiluliumas, whose name means "he from the place of the pure spring," was born a prince of the royal house of Hatti. His great-grandfather, Tudhaliyas II, ruled from 1460 to 1444 B.C., and his grandfather and father were also kings.

Scholars know little about the early life of Suppiluliumas. Most available information comes from the ruins of his city—located in central Turkey—and several thousand clay tablets found there. It is believed that the young prince spent his youth preparing to be a warrior-king by hunting lions and other animals, practicing with war tools in the courtyard of the palace, and

▲ **A Hittite stele dating to the 16th century B.C.**

Event: The rise of the Hittite people and their conflicts with Egypt.

Role: Suppiluliumas, king of Hatti, conquered neighboring Mediterranean city-states located in what is now northeastern Turkey, then continued south to battle for the cities of Carchemish and Amka near present-day Palestine. His expansion placed him in direct confrontation with the Egyptians, who wielded considerable influence in the Middle East in the middle of the fourteenth century B.C.

driving the three-man chariots of the Hittite army with their distinctive six spokes.

Suppiluliumas's reign began sometime before 1370 B.C. Compared with other kingdoms in the Middle East at the time, his Hatti empire was surprisingly democratic. While the pharaoh, or king, of Egypt was regarded as god and his word was considered law, the king of the Hittites inherited his position and his actions were subject to the approval of a council of nobles, the Pankus.

Participation: Expanding the Hittite Realm

First kingly steps. Suppiluliumas's rule was marked by an ongoing struggle against the Egyptians for control of land along the Mediterranean coast. Almost immediately after becoming king, he worked to strengthen the fortifications of the central city of Hattusas. Powerful armies began challenging the city from all sides sometime during the late 1300s B.C. The king ordered a new wall—one with two large towers overlooking an arched gate—be built around the southern and eastern borders of the city.

Within a year Suppiluliumas's army took to the field to stop the advance of the army of the Mitanni. Although the Hittites suffered one defeat at the hands of troops led by King Tushratta of the Mitanni, they fought steadily and valiantly, winning a long series of battles over the long run. The Hittites later attacked the Mitanni and other

The Earliest Hittite Kings and Years of Their Reigns	
Labarnas I	c. 1680-c. 1650 B.C. He founded the kingdom of Hatti.
Hattusilis	c. 1650-c. 1620 B.C.
Mursilis I	c. 1620-c. 1590 B.C.
Telipinus	c. 1525-c. 1500 B.C.
Tudhaliyas II	c. 1460-c. 1444 B.C. He was great-grandfather of Suppiluliumas I.

The Hittite term for their ruler was *tabarna*, a variation of the name Labarnas. As the empire's first king, Labarnas called himself "the great king," "the king of the Hatti land," "the hero," and "the favorite of the weather god." Later in the empire's history, the king's name was changed to a title meaning "My Sunship."

◄

Much of what is known about Suppiluliumas comes from thousands of clay tablets, such as these, found in the ruins of Hattusas.

peoples on the upper Tigris River and drove them east across the Euphrates into the land of the Hurrians.

Moral leadership. Suppiluliumas won approval from the Pankus and earned distinction for his wisdom, religious tolerance, high moral standing, and keen sense of justice. But the king's fair mindedness apparently did not extend to women. Suppiluliumas openly exploited women and even sealed treaties by giving his own sister and daughter in marriage to opposing rulers.

Expansion of the kingdom. Using royal women as gifts to seal treaties was only part of Suppiluliumas's plan to expand the land of the Hatti. The king's armies also pressed eastward to command the land around the upper Tigris and Euphrates Rivers. Suppiluliumas then turned his attention southward, taking the region of Aleppo (now northern coastal Syria) and the ancient trading city of Carchemish, on the upper Euphrates River, after an eight-day siege.

Victories in Syria. In territories that his army seized, Suppiluliumas installed rulers who were sure to pledge allegiance to him. In Aleppo and Carchemish, for example, his sons became kings. Other territories remained under the rule of local leaders after they had sworn to uphold the supremacy of the Hatti ruler.

As Suppiluliumas expanded his territory through war and diplomacy, first east then south, he also expanded his ideas about culture, government, and law. Everywhere the Hittites went, they borrowed from those they conquered. For example, they employed the wedge-shaped symbols of Middle Eastern cuneiform writing, shaping it to their own language. Suppiluliumas also adopted the policy of regional divisions of government from his conquests.

Continuing conquest. Suppiluliumas and another son, who followed him as ruler of the Hittites, persisted in battling the Egyptians for control of land along the Mediterranean coast. They also continued to move northward, finally taking such powerful peoples as the Mitanni under their rule. Suppiluliumas died around 1335 B.C., but the Hittite empire he ruled survived for nearly 150 more years.

In 1288 the Hittites, still at war with Egypt, fought one of the world's most famous battles. Egypt maintained control of the southern part of the eastern Mediterranean coast (present-day Israel and Lebanon), while the Hittites controlled the northern part of the coast. A large and strongly fortified Hittite city, Kadesh, lay near the coast about thirty-five miles north of Lebanon's border with Syria. There the great king of Egypt, Ramses II, took his army to battle the Hittites and their allies under King Muwatallis. Although historians claim that the battle was indecisive, one ancient author wrote of a great Egyptian victory. This story later became the subject of a poem that ends:

> Then the king hurried forward, on the Hittite host he flew,
>
> "for the sixth time that I charged them," says the king—and listen well,
>
> "like Baal in his strength, on their rearward, lo! I fell,
>
> And I killed them, none escaped me, and I slew, and slew, and slew."
>
> (*A History of the World in Story, Song, and Art,* p. 162)

It was one of the last great battles for the Hittites, marking the end of their expansion toward Egypt. By 1190 B.C. the old Hittite empire disappeared and its great capital, Hattusas, was once again burned to the ground.

For More Information

Garstang, John. *The Hittite Empire.* New York: Gordon, 1976.

Gurney, O. R. *The Hittites.* New York: Viking, 1991.

A History of the World in Story, Song, and Art. Boston: Houghton Mifflin, 1914.

Trever, A. A. *History of Ancient Civilization.* New York: Harcourt, 1936.

Moses

c. 1350-c. 1250 B.C.

Personal Background

Sources of information. Moses was a Jewish patriarch who is thought to have lived more than three thousand years ago. Most of what is known about him comes from the Bible, specifically the Old Testament books of Exodus, Leviticus, Numbers, and Deuteronomy. Greek (also called Hellenistic) Jewish historians such as Philo Judaeus and Flavius Josephus were the primary chroniclers of Moses' life. As contemporaries of Jesus Christ, they had access to ancient documents that have since been destroyed. The story of Moses is also told in the Koran, the holy book of the Muslim religion written in the seventh century A.D. However, no Egyptian records of Moses' existence have ever been unearthed.

Over the centuries the tales of Moses' life and deeds have probably been changed or exaggerated by storytellers. Because biographical facts about him were not compiled until more than twelve hundred years after his death, some observers doubt the accuracy of historical reports. A few scholars question his very existence, although some believe that the man himself was real and that his actions are accurately portrayed in biblical references. However, it may be that Moses was a mythical figure inserted in Hebrew stories to emphasize lessons about how people should conduct their lives.

Hebrews in Egypt. The Hebrews (a Semitic people from southwest Asia, also known as Israelites or the Children of Israel)

▲ **Moses**

Event: Reestablishing a Hebrew society.

Role: Moses led the Hebrews out of slavery in Egypt, organized their religious and civil traditions, and served as their lawgiver and prophet. The Ten Commandments, which he delivered to the Hebrews near Mount Sinai, formed the basis for the moral traditions of Western civilization.

migrated to Egypt several centuries before Moses was born. Around 1800 B.C. Abraham, an ancient Hebrew leader, broke with religious tradition and began the practice of believing in only one god. His son Isaac and grandson Jacob continued this custom, as did Jacob's sons. Joseph, the eleventh and most favored son of Jacob, became the victim of a family conspiracy that resulted in his being sold into slavery in Egypt. Thus began the historic movement of the Jews into Egyptian territory.

Several other factors, including famine, later led the rest of Abraham's ancestors to migrate to Egypt. Although they were initially welcomed, the Hebrews were eventually enslaved by the Egyptians, who "made their lives bitter with hard labor" (Exodus 1:4). Afraid that the Hebrews were becoming too numerous and powerful, one particularly cruel pharaoh, or Egyptian king, ordered all newborn baby boys of Jewish descent be drowned in the Nile River. It was around this time that Moses was born to Amram and Jochebed, members of the Hebrew tribe of Levi.

Myth or Truth?

While most students of history believe in the existence of the Hebrew leader Moses, the circumstances of his life remain unclear. The discovery of Assyrian stories of Sargon—a great king who lived about fifteen hundred years before the time of Moses—only deepen the mystery. Apparently, Sargon was saved from certain disaster as a baby by being placed in a basket near a river. This story bears a striking similarity to the one told about Moses in the Old Testament of the Bible.

The baby Moses. Fearing for her youngest child's safety, Moses' mother hid him as long as she could and later gave him up to save his life. She placed him in a basket, which she left in the reeds along the bank of the Nile River. The pharaoh's daughter discovered the basket and decided to adopt the Hebrew infant. "He became her son" (Exodus 2:10), and she gave him the Egyptian name Moses.

Moses grows up. As a member of the Egyptian nobility, Moses was given the finest education possible. He studied mathematics; hieroglyphics, the ancient Egyptian method of writing; and Egyptian, Babylonian, Assyrian, and Sumerian literature. A serious and enthusiastic student, Moses was able to "comprehend by his genius many different subjects" (Philo Judaeus, p. 5).

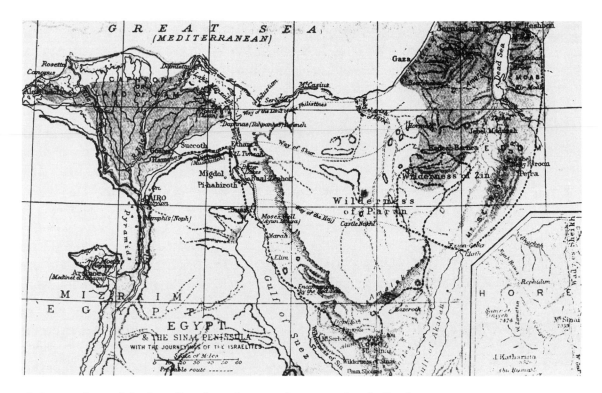

▲ Journeyings of the Israelites from Egypt to Canaan, a land "flowing with milk and honey" that had been promised to Hebrew leader Abraham five hundred years earlier.

Participation:
Leading the Hebrews out of Slavery

Concern for the Hebrews. Despite his high position in Egyptian society, Moses remained devoted to his fellow Hebrews and displayed a deep concern for their welfare. As noted in the writings of Philo Judaeus, he urged the Egyptian overseers to treat the slaves with moderation and "relax and abate somewhat the oppressive nature of their commands" (Philo Judaeus, p. 10).

Several Hebrew sources indicate that Moses risked his own life in the fight for justice for his people. After witnessing an Egyptian's savage attack on a Hebrew slave, for instance, Moses is said to have rushed to the Hebrew's defense. According to the Old Testament book of Exodus, he "avenged [the slave] by killing the Egyptian" (Exodus 2:12), and then hid the body in the sand. The pharaoh later heard about Moses' actions and ordered him killed.

Forced into exile. Moses fled east across the Sinai Peninsula and the Gulf of Aqaba to Midian in present-day Saudi Arabia. There he met and married Zipporah, whose father, a local priest, employed him as a sheep herder.

Moses lived in Midian for several years, raised a family, and continued to work as a shepherd. It was around this time, according to Scripture, that God appeared to him through the symbolic burning bush at Mount Horeb, also known as Mount Sinai. The book of Exodus details God's divine revelation to Moses. Chosen to lead the Hebrews out of bondage in Egypt, Moses was instructed by God to deliver his people to Canaan, also known as Palestine, an ancient region of southwest Asia lying to the northwest of Saudi Arabia. God had promised this land, which was "flowing with milk and honey" (Exodus 3:4), to Abraham more than five hundred years earlier.

Sources of Dissension

After the destruction of the Egyptian army in the Red Sea crossing, those Hebrews who had questioned Moses' authority began to see his leadership as part of God's grand design. But later, as they wandered through the desert hungry, thirsty, and tired, dissension broke out among the Israelites. During this time of crisis, some are actually said to have longed for their former slave status.

Initially, Moses felt that he lacked the power to fulfill God's command. But with divine grace, reassurance, and intervention, he set out on his mission to free the Hebrew slaves from Egypt, which was now ruled by a different pharaoh.

The dramatic return to Egypt. Moses used his staff to unleash a series of miraculous plagues on Egypt. The Nile River is said to have turned bloodred; frogs, gnats, flies, and grasshoppers overran Egypt; a deadly epidemic of anthrax plagued the livestock; and a hailstorm ravaged the land, only to be followed by three days of darkness. Still the pharaoh was unmoved.

Moses then declared that God would send a plague to kill the firstborn child of every Egyptian family, including the royal family. Only the Hebrews would be spared. This final act of devastation caused the pharaoh to relent; he allowed Moses to lead the slaves out of Egypt.

The Hebrew escape. After the Hebrews left, the pharaoh quickly realized their value as workers in Egyptian society and

▲ **Moses on Mount Sinai, receiving the Ten Commandments, laws that formed the basis for future Hebrew society.**

regretted granting his consent for their release. He sent an army to capture them and return them to bondage. At the Yam Suph, or "sea of reeds"—probably one of the lakes along the route of the present-day Suez Canal or the Red Sea—the soldiers caught up with the Hebrews.

According to historic accounts of the journey, Moses and his people executed a miraculous escape through the "sea of reeds." Moses stretched out his staff over the water, and "the Lord drove the sea back with a strong west wind.... The waters were divided and the Israelites went through the sea on dry ground with a wall of water on their right and on their left" (Exodus 14:21-22). When

The Ten Commandments

The laws of God's covenant with the Israelites, said to have been written on two stone tablets, have become known as the Ten Commandments.

The first four commandments serve to define the relationship between God and his people and establish the following as principles: the God of Israel is the one true God; worship of any other gods is not allowed; misuse of the name of God is not allowed; and the Sabbath day must be kept holy.

The rest of the commandments set forth basic social values and place limits on behavior: parents must be obeyed, and murder, adultery, stealing, giving false testimony, and coveting another person's goods (desiring something that belongs to someone else) are all prohibited.

In addition to these basic rules, Moses claimed to have received numerous laws, rules, and regulations covering property rights, criminal activities, social responsibilities, and religious practices. Punishments were designed to fit crimes. Thieves, for example, were required to pay back those from whom they stole. Crimes such as murder, kidnapping, cursing one's parents, and practicing witchcraft brought the death penalty.

the Egyptians pursued the Israelites through the water, Moses stretched out his hand and the sea rolled back to its place, drowning the Egyptian army.

The Hebrews wandered in the desert, guided, it is said, by a "pillar of cloud" by day and a "pillar of fire" by night (Exodus 19:16). By the time they arrived at Mount Sinai, they were hungry, weary, and frightened about their uncertain future. With their faith in God shaken, some even began to turn to the gods of their previous Egyptian lords for solace.

Three days after they set up camp at Sinai, a thunderstorm engulfed the mountain. At this point, according to Hebrew Scripture, God revealed himself to Moses and established a covenant, or agreement, with the Israelites. Moses then received the Ten Commandments—the conditions of the covenant between God and the people. These laws, which the Israelites readily adopted, formed the basis for future Hebrew society.

Aftermath

Wandering the desert. After departing Egypt, the Israelites wandered in the desert for forty years before reaching Canaan. These decades of uncertainty were said to be a punishment for the Hebrew people's lack of faith in both God's revelations and Moses' leadership. According to Old Testament Scripture, the Hebrews who fled from Egypt died during those forty long years. However, their descendants, a new generation of Israelites raised from childhood under the new laws and commandments, were later allowed to enter the land promised to Abraham. Eventually they moved into what is now Jordan and conquered the land west of the Jordan River.

Moses' death. Moses never entered the Promised Land. He died before the Israelites, under the leadership of his successor, Joshua, conquered Canaan. Reflecting on the importance of Moses' legacy to the course of modern civilization, American philosopher Russell Kirk suggested, "Our modern moral order, at least in what is called the West, runs back to the burning bush on Sinai" (Kirk, p. 17).

Mount Sinai

The location of Mount Sinai is unclear. It is traditionally believed to be Gabal Musa (Mount Moses) in the southern Sinai Peninsula. However, some scholars, noting the biblical descriptions of smoke and fire, believe Mount Sinai is in northwestern Saudi Arabia, where volcanoes were once active.

For More Information

Kirk, Russell. *The Roots of American Order*. 3rd edition. Washington, D.C.: Regnery Gateway, 1991.

Noerlinger, Henry S. *Moses and Egypt: The Documentation for the Motion Picture "The Ten Commandments."* Los Angeles: University of Southern California Press, 1956.

Philo Judaeus. *The Works of Philo Judaeus, the Contemporary of Josephus.* Translated by C. D. Yonge. London: Henry G. Bohn, 1855.

The Student Bible. New International Version. Grand Rapids, Michigan: Zondervan, 1992.

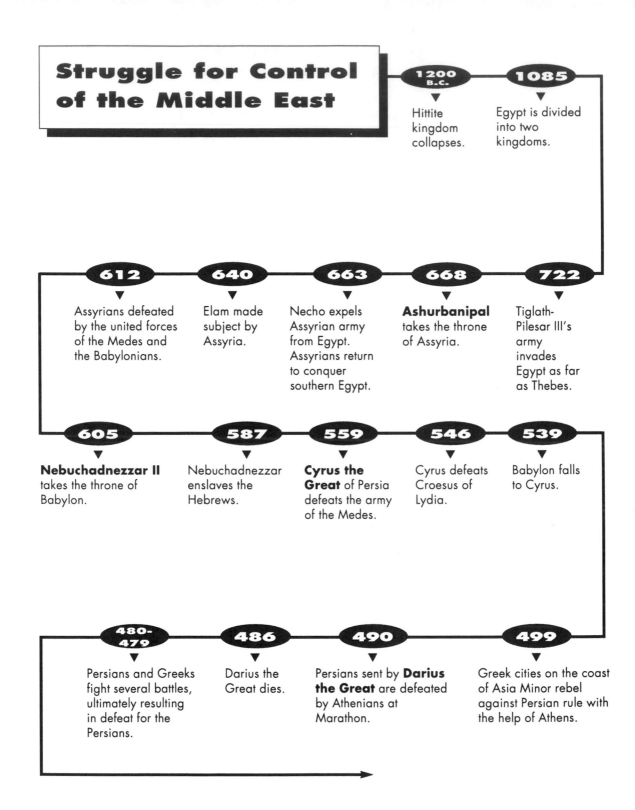

Struggle for Control of the Middle East

1200 B.C. — Hittite kingdom collapses.

1085 — Egypt is divided into two kingdoms.

722 — Tiglath-Pilesar III's army invades Egypt as far as Thebes.

668 — **Ashurbanipal** takes the throne of Assyria.

663 — Necho expels Assyrian army from Egypt. Assyrians return to conquer southern Egypt.

640 — Elam made subject by Assyria.

612 — Assyrians defeated by the united forces of the Medes and the Babylonians.

605 — **Nebuchadnezzar II** takes the throne of Babylon.

587 — Nebuchadnezzar enslaves the Hebrews.

559 — **Cyrus the Great** of Persia defeats the army of the Medes.

546 — Cyrus defeats Croesus of Lydia.

539 — Babylon falls to Cyrus.

499 — Greek cities on the coast of Asia Minor rebel against Persian rule with the help of Athens.

490 — Persians sent by **Darius the Great** are defeated by Athenians at Marathon.

486 — Darius the Great dies.

480–479 — Persians and Greeks fight several battles, ultimately resulting in defeat for the Persians.

STRUGGLE FOR CONTROL OF THE MIDDLE EAST

While China and Egypt had grown under single rulers for more than one thousand years, the Middle East had formed and re-formed many separate states, each in turn attempting to dominate the entire area. To some extent, the difference in development in the Middle East was due to geography.

The earliest civilization in the region was that of the Sumerians. Their capital was located at Agade, not far from the Persian Gulf. To the north, where the Tigris and Euphrates Rivers grow farther apart, sat an extremely fertile region of middle land. With proper canals for irrigation, the area between and just across the rivers supported lush grain fields much like those in Egypt.

Babylon, a farm-village turned city, was the nucleus of another kingdom, although it was not always inhabited or controlled by the same peoples. The Babylonian trade center attracted immigrants from throughout the region.

The city of Babylon was surrounded by mountains. At one time, to the east, the nation of Elam flourished in the nearby Zagros Mountains, which today provide protection to the rebellious Kurds of Iran and Iraq. North of Babylon, where the river valleys give way to rocky, rolling plains broken by mountain ridges, lived the Assyrians and, deeper into the mountains, the

Medes. Around 1800 B.C., the Hittite empire was founded to the west, in present-day Turkey. The Hittites eventually moved toward the Euphrates River and captured Carchemish, an ancient trading center that grew into a key hub of power in the region.

Egypt. Located in the southwestern portion of the Middle East, Egypt is somewhat isolated by the desert of the Sinai Peninsula and by the Mediterranean Sea. But the ties between that nation and the coastal trading areas of present-day Palestine, Lebanon, and Syria have existed for centuries. Egyptians, Babylonians, Assyrians, and Hittites each at one time or another tried to control the smaller coastal kingdoms in the region—most notably, the kingdom of Judah.

Hatti, Babylonia, and Assyria. In the 1700s B.C., the Hittite empire grew to great strength and then began to fade. Ancient Egypt had also begun to lose its power. Babylon, under its great early lawgiver Hammurabi, became the major force in the Middle East and remained prominent, despite the attacks of Assyrians, Medes, and Elamites, for nearly one thousand years.

Then, around 700 B.C., a great king united the small kingdoms of the north under the rule of the Assyrians. Tiglath-Pilesar III invaded and destroyed the Babylonian empire. Under his rule, the Assyrians then marched along the Mediterranean coast and across the desert to attack a divided Egypt. For a while, Assyria controlled both Babylon and the delta area of Egypt. But Babylon was not easily governed from a distance. Successive Assyrian rulers, weary of the city's resistance, completely destroyed it. Within ten years, however, Babylon was rebuilt.

A plan for peace between Assyria and Babylon was devised by an Assyrian ruler in the late 600s B.C. He named one of his sons, **Ashurbanipal,** successor to the throne of Assyria and made another son the king of Babylon. The plan worked for more than a decade. Ashurbanipal was able to rebound from defeat at the hands of a new Egyptian leader, Necho, and retake Egyptian territory. After a peaceful and cooperative sixteen years, however, his brother in Babylon attempted a rebellion with the help of the Elamites. Although that rebellion was thwarted, it encouraged further Elamite attacks on Assyria. In 612 B.C., only a few years after Ashurbanipal's death, the Assyrian empire fell to a union of mountain people led by a new power, the Medes.

The new Babylon. Seven years later Babylon was revived under a powerful ruler from Chaldea, **Nebuchadnezzar II,** to again dominate the Middle East. Taking the throne in 605 B.C., the new king of Babylon worked to recapture control of the small Mediterranean trading states once dominated by Assyria and Egypt. A year later he headed an army to overtake Egyptian forces far north and chase them back into Egypt. By 587 B.C., having tired of the rebellions of Judah, he invaded that small nation, taking as many as four thousand Hebrews prisoner and making them slaves in Babylon.

Syria. Babylon's dominance, however, was doomed by the expansions of **Cyrus the Great,** who ruled a small Persian city-state. Cyrus first took control of Susa, the capital of Elam. Then, sweeping north and west, his armies overtook the Medes at Ecbatana and attacked and defeated the famous king of Lydia, Croesus, in what is now Turkey. Around 539 B.C. he seized Babylon, which by this time was wracked by internal strife. Cyrus had gained control of the northern Middle East and sought to add Egypt to his kingdom, but he died before he could carry out his plan. His son finished his work, capturing Egypt for Persian rule.

Still flexing its military muscle, Persia, led by Cyrus's grandson **Darius the Great,** prepared to add parts of Greece to its conquests. But Persian forces on land and sea suffered a bitter defeat on Greek soil under Darius. The loss in the Persian Wars began the weakening of Persia. The empire would remain a formidable power for another 150 years, until it would finally be destroyed by a Greek leader from Macedonia, Alexander the Great.

The fight for control of the Middle East during the first millennium B.C. generated massive social and political change among the regions' various peoples. Through their struggles to dominate and rule a very diverse population, the leaders of the Middle East left a legacy of established laws, principles of government, and moral codes. In addition, their deep respect for learning and cultural preservation is reflected in the great libraries found at Nineveh, Babylon, Hattusas, and several cities in Egypt.

Ashurbanipal

c. 688-627 B.C.

Personal Background

Ancient Assyria. The Middle East has been a politically and culturally turbulent region for more than three thousand years. During the seventh century B.C., Nineveh, the leading center of trade in ancient Assyria, lay to the north on the eastern side of the Tigris River, while Babylon, the area's old cultural center, sat farther south on the banks of the Euphrates River near the Persian Gulf. These two city-states, each with a dozen or two lesser cities loyal to them, had quarreled often for more than a century. Successive kings of Assyria had driven their armies across the Middle East, and by the time Ashurbanipal came to power, the Assyrians of Nineveh dominated the two river valleys. They had taken control of the land from the Persian Gulf to the headwaters of the two great rivers and from the Mediterranean into the land that is now Iran.

Over the years. Kings of Nineveh had marched against Babylon and captured the city over and over again, but the Babylonians always seemed able to recover and recapture at least some of their independence. Ashurbanipal's grandfather, Sennacherib, tried to put an end to the constant battling by totally destroying the old city. Only ten years later, his son Esarhaddon, the new king of Assyria, ordered the city restored to its original beauty and established a palace there, as well as one in Nineveh.

▲ **Ashurbanipal**

Event: Expanding the influence of Assyria.

Role: Taking the reign of Assyria upon his father's death, Ashurbanipal expanded the kingdom to rule over much of the Middle East. He built the capital city of Nineveh into one of the cultural centers of the ancient world and organized the region's first library.

Nineveh. In the early nineteenth century A.D., scientists began exploring several large mounds of earth near the present-day city of Mosul, Iraq. There on the east bank of the Tigris River nearly twenty-five hundred years earlier, the reigning King Sennacherib had built up the Assyrian capital city. Nineveh grew into a great walled community shaped like a trapezoid, its main entrance featuring a gate decorated with man-headed bulls and winged human statues. Nearly one mile of alabaster and limestone carvings adorned the wall on either side of the entrance. Inside the fortified city lived as many as two hundred thousand people, led by a king who claimed the right to rule through the god Assur and the goddess Ishtar.

A small portion of the eighteen-hundred-acre city was reserved for the king's palace. Enclosed by yet another wall, the palace was far more than just the royal residence: it functioned as the center of business and political activity for the whole kingdom and included a main trading center, government offices, and the training grounds for the king's large army.

The sons of Esarhaddon. Around 680 B.C. King Sennacherib was killed, and the kingdom was left to his son Esarhaddon. Esarhaddon and his wife had two sons, Ashurbanipal and Shamashshumuken. Both boys were prepared early in life to take on the roles of fearless warriors. They practiced using bows and arrows and swords, rode on horseback, and became skilled in the operation of two-wheeled chariots.

Babylon. For centuries Babylon had been recognized as the center of culture in the Middle East. Conquerors before Ashurbanipal's grandfather, Sennacherib, had respected its importance and arranged for it to be a "free city"—exempt from various trade

The Growth of Assyria

783-745 B.C.	Tiglath-Pilesar IV takes control of Palestine and Phoenicia.
745-734 B.C.	King Nabonassar captures Babylon.
734-705 B.C.	King Sargon II captures Israel and scatters the Hebrews throughout the empire. He then expands south and east to capture the kingdom of Elam.
705-680 B.C.	King Sennacherib, upset with the rebirth of Babylon, attacks and destroys the city. Nineveh is built into the capital city of the Assyrians.

▲ Bas relief, possibly of a royal banquet, from the palace at Nineveh; Ashurbanipal built the city into one of the cultural centers of the ancient world.

rules and from some Assyrian taxes. Babylonians were quick to take advantage of this favored status and often maneuvered for complete Babylonian independence by mounting armed rebellions against the Assyrians. An aging Esarhaddon took steps to strengthen the Assyrian hold on Babylonia by appointing his second son, Shamashshumuken, king of Babylon. He had already chosen Ashurbanipal to be co-ruler of Assyria.

Participation:
The Assyrian-Babylonian Conflict

Early reign. Ashurbanipal took the throne at a time when many lesser kingdoms were challenging the rule of Nineveh. The Assyrians had conquered much of the land in southwest Asia and even extended their influence into what is now the northeast

African republic of Egypt. Ashurbanipal's first few years as king were spent putting down rebellions—particularly in Egypt, where he led his army against rebel leader Tirhaga and defeated him, only to find the Egyptians rallying behind another warrior, Psammeticus. Under Psammeticus, Egypt regained its independence for a while, but in 663 B.C. Ashurbanipal and the Assyrians completely conquered the Egyptians.

For the next sixteen years, Nineveh was more or less at peace, and Ashurbanipal had time to beautify his palace, make stronger trade arrangements, erect monuments commemorating his accomplishments, and, most importantly, supervise his scribes in the compilation of historical tales about him.

The Assyrian kings were experts in using written propaganda to keep their enemies on edge. Ashurbanipal's grandfather had been a master at instilling fear through the work of his scribes. "I built a pillar against [my enemy's] city gate," went one such story. "Some I walled up within the pillar, some I impaled upon the pillar on stakes ... and I cut off the limbs of the officers" (Kramer, p. 58).

Names in Ancient Assyria

Members of the ruling Assyrian family often took names representing the god to whom they paid primary allegiance. Claiming to be made king under the god Assur, the ruler in the seventh century B.C. took the name Ashurbanipal; his main wife took the name Ashursharrat. (Assyrian society was very male-dominated. The chief wife took a name related to that of her husband but was not called "queen." Rather, Ashursharrat was known as "she-of-the palace.")

Shamashshumuken. Babylon was an old city by Ashurbanipal's time. It had long been a center of study and trade for the entire Middle East. Even though the city was subject to the king at Nineveh, its people were free to carry on trade anywhere in the world. Even so, Shamashshumuken—Ashurbanipal's younger brother, who ruled as king of Babylon—wanted more power. Throughout the early 660s and the 650s B.C., Shamashshumuken was busy forging political and military ties with kings of nearby regions such as the southwest kingdoms of Elam (present-day Iran) and Arabia. By 650 B.C. he and his allies revolted.

Ashurbanipal was so angered by his brother's rebellious plot that he gathered his army and attacked Babylon. Again the city

▲ Ashurbanipal seated on his throne holding a cup of wine in his right hand; behind him is an attendant with a fly swatter and the royal bow, quiver, and sword.

▲ Seventh-century B.C. stone carving of Ashurbanipal spearing a lion; the Assyrian kingdom was so tightly controlled that Ashurbanipal was able to spend much of his time at his favorite sport.

was destroyed. Next he turned his attention toward Arabia and Elam, crushing both of those kingdoms as well.

Recordkeeper. Aside from his military conquests, Ashurbanipal is remembered for his great devotion to the arts. During his reign, he founded the first great library at Nineveh. After the destruction of Babylon, he ordered his scribes to copy many of the tablets rescued from that city's great library for inclusion in Nineveh's archives.

In the mid-ninteenth century British archaeologists began to explore the site of ancient Nineveh. Teams of diggers uncovered clay tablets covered with wedge-shaped marks known as cuneiform writing. These finds have been identified as records from the great library founded by Ashurbanipal. Many of the more than twenty-five thousand unearthed tablets are now housed in the British Museum.

Aftermath

The fall of Assyria. For more than forty years, Ashurbanipal ruled Assyria and held the thousand-mile-long empire together. When he died in 627 B.C., the empire remained fairly strong but was beginning to show the strains of age. Ashurbanipal was succeeded by his son, who ruled for only three years before being replaced by an uncle. Neither of these rulers was strong enough to keep a firm grip on the kingdom.

Babylon, a staunch and longtime enemy, led the revolt that finally destroyed the Assyrian empire. Nabopolassar, the Babylonian king at the time, had formed an alliance with Cyaxares, king of the Medes, a growing power in the Middle East. Together, the two began to conquer one part of Assyria after another until Nineveh itself was besieged. The strong walls of the city withstood the first attacks, but eventually the city was overrun and destroyed by fire, with its last king, Sinsariskun, dying in the flames.

For More Information

Bibby, Geoffrey. *Looking for Dilmun.* New York: Alfred A. Knopf, 1969.

Kramer, Samuel Noah, and the editors of Time-Life Books. *Cradle of Civilization.* New York: Time, 1967.

Layard, Henry Austen. *Nineveh and Its Remains.* New York: Praeger, 1970.

Oppenheim, A. Leo. *Ancient Mesopotamia: Portrait of a Dead Civilization.* Chicago: University of Chicago Press, 1964.

Ashurbanipal the Hunter

Ashurbanipal's father had conquered an empire that stretched from the Persian Gulf to present-day Turkey and along the east coast of the Mediterranean Sea to include Egypt. After a few more years of fighting, the Assyrian kingdom was so tightly controlled that Ashurbanipal was able to spend much of his time at his favorite activity: lion-hunting:

> In my sport I seized ... a fierce lion of the plain by his ears. With the aid of [the gods] Assur and Ishtar ... I pierced his body with my lance. Upon the lions which I slew, I rested the fierce bow of the goddess Ishtar. I offered a sacrifice over them and poured on them a libation of wine. (Kramer, pp. 66-68)

Nebuchadnezzar II

c. 630-562 B.C.

Personal Background

Babylon, Assyria, and the Medes. Nebuchadnezzar II was probably the most famous of all the kings of Babylon. His father, Nabopolassar, began his own rule in the city as satrap, or territorial under-ruler, for the king of Assyria. Later, as the king of Babylon, Nabopolassar joined forces with the Medes, a rising power of the north country, to defeat the Assyrians. Twenty years after the death of **Ashurbanipal** (see entry), the last great Assyrian king, Babylon became an independent nation. Nabopolassar then set out to conquer most of the land that had once been claimed by Assyria. He also struck a bargain with the Median king that guaranteed Babylonian freedom: he promised that his son, Nebuchadnezzar II, would marry Amuhia, the princess of the Medes.

Nebuchadnezzar II. Not much is known about Nebuchadnezzar's youth, but he was probably trained early on for a life as a war leader and hunter. As a young prince, he also learned to read and write. He was schooled in the language of Babylon, known as Akkadian, and in the form of writing used at the time—a system of triangular marks in clay tablets called cuneiform writing.

Nebuchadnezzar's inheritance. Nabopolassar and Nebuchadnezzar were not Assyrians or members of the ancient families of Babylon. Rather, they were descendants of tribesmen who

▲ **Nebuchadnezzar II**

Event: Making Babylon a cultural center.

Role: Following in his father's footsteps, Nebuchadnezzar II expanded Babylonian territory and developed the city of Babylon into the cultural center of the Middle East.

had farmed and herded cattle in the swampland nearer the Persian Gulf. These people, known as Chaldeans, gradually united into a strong force in the region, eventually found their way to Babylon, and became powerful enough to take over the government there.

Nabopolassar was the first Chaldean king of Babylon. He and the king of the Medes had agreed to divide ancient Assyria. Media would take the north land between the two rivers and Babylon would rule over the Mediterranean coastal lands of Syria, ancient Phoenicia, Palestine, and Egypt. An Egyptian leader named Necho, however, refused to accept this division. Necho laid claim to Egypt and then moved north toward Phoenicia. In 605 B.C. Nebuchadnezzar was sent by his father to tame Necho, but by that time Necho had already crushed Judah (an area now divided between the Middle Eastern territories of Israel and Jordan) and was moving along the seacoast to the old Assyrian empire.

The Chaldean Kings of Babylonia and Years of Their Reigns	
Nabopolassar	625-605 B.C.
Nebuchadnezzar II	605-562 B.C.
Awil-Marduk	561-560 B.C.
Neriglissar	559-556 B.C.
Labashi-Marduk	556 B.C.
Nabu-na'id	555-539 B.C.

The battle of Carchemish. King Necho swiftly took possession of all the lands along the eastern Mediterranean coast—a task made easier by nations such as Judah, whose people had long preferred being subject to Egypt rather than to the Assyrians and Babylonians. With their help Necho approached the Euphrates River near the place where it now crosses into Turkey. Carchemish, the longtime trade center in what is now northern Syria, seemed to be his goal.

Nebuchadnezzar's army met with the Egyptians in a fierce battle at Carchemish, beating Necho and his soldiers so thoroughly that the Babylonians were able to drive them back into Egypt and, in the process, recapture Judah and the Jewish people. Nebuchadnezzar was moving toward Egypt when he received word that his father had died. The prince rushed home to Babylon to take the throne.

The Jews. The kingdom of Judah mounted three unsuccessful rebellions against the Babylonians. Each skirmish resulted in the deportation of some Judeans to different regions of the Baby-

▲ Remains of the great palaces of Babylon; Nebuchadnezzar developed the city into the cultural center of the Middle East.

lonian empire. Finally, around 587 B.C., the Babylonian army entered Jerusalem, captured Jehoiachin, the king, and took him along with four thousand Jews into captivity in Babylon. The rest of the citizens of Judah were left to be ruled by Zedekiah, a puppet king (one who rules in name only).

Participation: Building Babylon

With peace restored, Nebuchadnezzar was able to turn his attention to making Babylon one of the world's leading cultural sites. The city was already thousands of years old when the king

▲ The ziggurat at Ur, which Nebuchadnezzar ordered rebuilt to make it the tallest building in the empire.

decided to develop it as an urban model. Located on the east bank of the Euphrates River, the walled community included a river port for trade, a royal palace, and temples to the various gods, along with rows of houses for the craftsmen of the kingdom. Canals ran out from the river around the city, where farmers lived in huts and raised barley and wheat.

Nebuchadnezzar's palace consisted of five large courtyards surrounded by the buildings for a garrison of soldiers, state offices, and the homes of government officials. Near the palace, the great Ishtar Gate joined the royal entryway into the city with a sixty-six-foot-wide main street bearing the name "May the enemy not have victory."

The new city. Nebuchadnezzar expanded his city across the Euphrates River. A new section as large as the old city was built on the waterway's west bank, and a masonry bridge was erected to span the river and connect the two halves of the city. Eventually, Babylon grew to cover nearly three thousand acres within its massive walls; its population is estimated to have been about two to three hundred thousand.

In the desert land of Babylonia, plants could be grown only with the help of irrigation systems. Nebuchadnezzar extended the networks of canals that brought water to the fields. By the time of his death, it is believed that he had upgraded Babylon's entire canal system and erected outposts to guard both the city and the farmland—an area of some four hundred square miles.

In 1899 German scientists began exploring the area of ancient Babylon, about fifty miles south of present-day Baghdad in Iraq. From that time until the dawn of World War I, the explorers carefully uncovered the ruins of the once-great city. Babylon had been built of a combination of mud and fire-hardened bricks. As the city aged, these bricks were scattered in mud and silt, and some of them had been carried off by Iranians to construct new buildings in other places.

The Tower of Babel

Near Nebuchadnezzar's palace stood the old ziggurat, an ancient temple reserved for sacrifices and worship to the main god, Marduk-Bel. Nebuchadnezzar ordered the three-story temple rebuilt so that it would be the tallest building in the empire, a "house of the platform of Heaven and Earth" (Saggs, p. 5). A mixture of clay and brick, the tower ended up being seven stories and three hundred feet in height, with stairways thirty feet wide rising to the third story. (How the Babylonians got from the third floor to the seventh remains a mystery.)

Some historians claim that the Babylonian ziggurat was the original Tower of Babel described in the Bible. According to the Old Testament book of Genesis, construction of the tower led to what is known as "the confusion of languages." Babylon was perhaps as ethnically mixed as any of the old cities. Hurrians, Armenians, Chaldeans, Egyptians, Hittites, Elamites, and Jews were only a few of the people who lived there at one time or another.

Aftermath

For four years during his reign, Nebuchadnezzar was unable to rule. Ancient scripture suggests that he went temporarily insane, crawling around the city and eating grass as animals did. Regardless of what happened at this time, he eventually returned to work,

▲ Seventeenth-century engraving depicting the capture of Jerusalem.
Around 587 B.C., Nebuchadnezzar's army entered the city, captured the
king, and took him and four thousand Jews into captivity in Babylon.

ruling his kingdom for a total of forty-three years. Nebuchadnezzar died in 562 B.C., after building Babylon into one of the most impressive of the ancient cities.

The fall of Babylon. Nebuchadnezzar's son inherited the Babylonian kingdom but was assassinated after ruling for only two years. Other relatives followed as kings, but with little success. By 539 B.C. the contenders for the rule of Babylon were involved in so much quarreling that Persia, a new power led by **Cyrus the Great** (see entry), was able to enter the city and claim it without any serious opposition. Babylon then became a city within the new and powerful empire of the Persians.

For More Information

Fagan, Brian M. *Return to Babylon.* Boston: Little, Brown, 1979.

Lissner, Ivar. *The Living Past.* New York: Van Rees, 1957.

Oppenheim, A. Leo. *Ancient Mesopotamia: Portrait of a Dead Civilization.* Chicago: University of Chicago Press, 1964.

Oppenheim, A. Leo. *Letters from Mesopotamia.* Chicago: University of Chicago Press, 1967.

Saggs, H. W. F. *The Greatness That Was Babylon.* New York: Hawthorn Books, 1962.

The Hanging Gardens

Legend has it that Nebuchadnezzar ordered the construction of the hanging gardens—one of the "seven wonders of the ancient world"—to ease his wife's longing for the mountains and forests of her native land to the north. Soil was placed in tiers atop an arched building, and trees and other plants were grown for the queen's pleasure. Special waterways carried water from the river to these "hanging" gardens.

Cyrus the Great

c. 600-c. 529 B.C.

Personal Background

The Middle East. According to scholars, most ancient rulers of the Middle East directed their scribes to write glowing accounts of their accomplishments—accounts that would leave no question as to the validity of their claim to the throne. But the early histories of rulers such as Cyrus II, known as the Great, are largely the product of myth and unsupported stories. One of the best reports about Cyrus was written in the fifth century B.C. by Herodotus, a Greek scholar who came to be known as the "Father of History."

The birth of Cyrus. Three powerful nations controlled most of the Middle East in the sixth century B.C. Nebuchadnezzar ruled over Babylon and demanded the allegiance of more than a dozen lesser kings; Croesus ruled the rich land of Lydia, located in modern-day Syria; and in the northeast, Astyages reigned over the powerful kingdom of the Medes. One of the lesser territories that paid allegiance and money to Media was Elam, which lay to the south. Astyages put his son-in-law, a Persian named Cambyses, in charge of this subkingdom. Cambyses' son, Cyrus, is believed to have been born in a town called Anzan (now Murghab in present-day Iran) around 600 B.C.

The myth of Cyrus's childhood. According to the old stories written by Herodotus and other historians, King Astyages was plagued by a series of disturbing dreams that led him to

▲ **Cyrus the Great**

Event: The unification of the Persian Empire.

Role: Conquering first the Median kingdom, then the smaller city-states along the Mediterranean Sea, and finally Babylon, Cyrus the Great became the first ruler of the Persian Empire (centered in present-day Iran). His just treatment of all those he conquered earned him the names "Father of the People" in Persia and the "Liberator" among the Jews.

▲ **Cyrus the Great leading his troops in battle; Cyrus was so fair to those he conquered that he earned distinction among Middle Eastern leaders.**

regret the very birth of his grandson Cyrus. In the first dream, he was supposedly told that Cyrus would bring great danger to the kingdom of the Medes. Another dream revealed that the youth would replace him as ruler of the Medes. A frantic Astyages ordered one of his most trusted soldiers, Harpagus, to kill Cyrus.

Harpagus could not bring himself to kill a baby of the royal family. Instead he took Cyrus to one of his sheepherders; the herdsman and his wife adopted the child and raised him to be a herder. But Cyrus's royal ancestry soon became apparent through his words and actions. When Astyages learned that his grandson was still alive, he took revenge on Harpagus, killing his son.

Conquering the Medes. Astyages did not threaten Cyrus's life again until the boy had grown and replaced his father as king of the Persians. The aged Astyages then decided that the Persian threat was too serious to ignore and sent his army against Cyrus. The two met in a great battle in 559 B.C., and the army of the Medes was soundly defeated by the upstart Persians—with the help of the old soldier, Harpagus.

Afterward, according to the old historical accounts, Cyrus displayed such fairness in his actions that he earned distinction among Middle Eastern leaders: instead of killing Astyages or forcing him to renounce all of his wealth, Cyrus allowed the old ruler to live in his palace and appointed him special adviser to the king. Cyrus then reigned as king of both Media and Persia. He built a city, Pasar-gadae, and a palace on the site of the battle with Astyages. Today the ruin of his capital city lies in the mountains northeast of the modern Iranian city of Shiraz. An unusual capital for its day, Pasargadae was protected by the mountains rather than by man-made walls.

Oracles

In the sixth century B.C. it was customary to travel to one of three sacred, monastery-like places to ask the gods important questions. Their answers, or oracles, were delivered by priests or priestesses who presided over the questioning. The procedure went something like this: A rich man might go to or send a messenger to a priest or priestess with a special sacrifice—perhaps a goat of a certain age. The goat would be killed and fed to the priest. Its skin would then be placed in front of an altar, and the king or his messenger would lie down upon it to ask the questions. Then, when the questioner became sleepy, the oracle would be given through the priest or priestess.

Participation: Building the Persian Empire

Croesus. West of Cyrus's growing kingdom lay the Mediterranean nation of Lydia, which contained mountains and river

▲ After he captured Babylon, Cyrus freed the Hebrews who were held there as slaves.

sands rich in gold deposits. Croesus, Lydia's king, was one of the wealthiest men in the world at the time. But he feared that Cyrus was becoming too powerful and might decide to conquer his kingdom and its capital city, Sardis (near what is now Smyrna in Turkey). Croesus set out to conquer Persia, but not before consulting the oracles—proclamations given by a deity through a priest or priestess—to see if he would be victorious.

Legend tells us that Croesus chose a crafty priestess to deliver the answer to his question. She spoke the oracles in verse and gave advice in the form of riddles. Her answer to Croesus's question about whether he would lose his throne to the Persians was: "Whene'er a mule shall mount upon the Median throne, then and not till then, shall the great Croesus fear to lose his own" (Lamb, pp. 55-56).

The fall of Lydia. Based on that response, Croesus felt sure that he would never lose his power to Cyrus. Still, to ensure victory, he hired Thales, a great Greek mathematician, to plan the march on Persia. He also wrote to the people of Sparta praising them as the strongest of the Greek armies and asking for their help. Neither of these acts helped Croesus's cause, however; Cyrus had already learned of his plan and was marching toward him. In 546 B.C. the two armies fought on even terms until by trickery Cyrus was able to enter Croesus's capital city and take the rich king captive.

Building Persia. One after another, the lesser kingdoms submitted to Cyrus until he controlled an area from present-day Pakistan to the Mediterranean Sea. Only one major kingdom, Babylon, stood in the way of his controlling all of the Middle East.

But after the death of the great Babylonian king Nebuchadnezzar, the city fell into weak hands and became the perfect target for a takeover. In 539 B.C. Cyrus's army entered Babylon and conquered it without much resistance. Babylon then became a mere secondary capital, and gradually the wonder of the city disappeared.

The Hebrews. Soon after taking Babylon, Cyrus freed the Hebrews who were being held there as slaves and allowed them to return to their native country, Judah. Cyrus also helped them rebuild the great temple in Jerusalem that Nebuchadnezzar had destroyed. Deeds such as these gained Cyrus the respect of all the people he ruled. It is said that Persians called him the "Father of the People," and Jews knew him as the "Liberator." The Jewish prophet Isaiah reportedly said Cyrus was "anointed of the Lord."

> ## Cyrus and the Hebrews
>
> Some of the little we know about the rule of Cyrus comes to us from biblical reports. The book of Isaiah describes Cyrus's commitment to rebuilding Jerusalem, and the book of Daniel tells of Daniel's experiences during the rule of Cyrus and Darius I.

Aftermath

At the height of his reign, Cyrus ruled the Middle East from the Hellespont (in northwest Turkey) to India. It was the largest empire ever to be established in the West and was governed differently than the kingdoms of Assyria and Babylon. The vast land

of Persia—with all its different ethnic groups—was divided into twenty-one provinces, each governed by a local leader called a satrap. This leader's loyalty to the king was ensured by the watchful eye of the royal secretary and military officer assigned to each province. In addition, special inspectors, "the eyes and ears of the king," traveled constantly through the kingdom (Wallbank, Taylor, and Bailkey, p. 59). Cyrus had roads built throughout the kingdom and organized his own "pony express" type system of communication to carry messages from one capital to another.

The Legacy of Cyrus the Great

Cyrus the Great left the West a new model for government. It has been said that:

1. He respected the religion of all people.
2. He destroyed no towns.
3. He killed no captor leaders.

Over the next decade, a new group known as the Scythians began rising to the northeast of the Caspian Sea. Only a small neighboring tribe in Cyrus's childhood, the Scythians had grown in numbers and in fierceness, spreading from Iran to occupy much of present-day Romania and western Russia. Ten years after his capture of Babylon, Cyrus was killed in battle by this new power. Nevertheless, the organization of the Persian Empire was so sound that Cyrus's son, Cambyses, was able to reorganize the army, conquer Egypt, and add it to the territory. Cambyses' successor to the Persian throne, **Darius the Great** (see entry), tried to continue the expansion of the empire by invading Greece, but his army and navy met with disaster and were totally defeated by a smaller Greek army.

For More Information

Lamb, Harold. *Cyrus the Great.* Garden City, New York: Doubleday, 1960.

Myers, Philip Van Ness. *Ancient History.* New York: Ginn, 1904.

Wallbank, T. Walter, Alastair M. Taylor, and Nels M. Bailkey. *Civilization: Past and Present.* 5th edition. Chicago: Scott, Foresman, 1965.

Wooley, Sir Leonard. *The Beginnings of Civilization.* New York: Mentor Books, 1965.

◄

Cyrus the Great restoring to his new subjects the religious treasures Babylon had taken from them.

Darius the Great

550-486 B.C.

Personal Background

His own story. A little more than fifty miles northeast of the modern city of Shiraz, Iran, is a pass through the Zagros Mountains that has long been called the gateway of Asia. About twenty-five hundred years ago, one of the world's most successful rulers founded a new capital city for his empire there and called it Persepolis. Darius I, the builder of Persepolis, who later earned the title Darius the Great, chose the rocky cliffs of this region for the site of his grave. The grave is decorated with scenes of royal life and images of the various peoples he ruled. Another cliff, located more than two hundred feet above the mountain chain's ancient roadway, bears carvings of events from Darius's life and a complete history of his accomplishments in cuneiform writing.

Early life. Darius was born in 550 B.C., the son of Hystaspes of the royal Achaemenid family, but little else is known of his early life. Herodotus, the great Greek world traveler, historian, and chronicler, suggested that young Persian noblemen were taught just three subjects: horsemanship, archery, and truthfulness. In addition, Darius must have had some religious training. He seems to have been a follower of the religion founded by Zoroaster in the seventh century B.C. More detailed accounts of the life of Darius begin with his twenty-eighth year.

Becoming king of Persia. Around 522 B.C. Cambyses, the king of Persia, committed suicide, leaving no clear successor to

DARIVS NOTHVS PERS REX

Perse iugulato, ac cineribus suffocato Sogdiano, per Arme-
niæ et Ægypti præfectos, et regni primates diadema sibi im-
posuit Darius Nothus. Interim Nehemias secundâ fun-
gens præfecturâ contemptu à se in priori edita decre-
ta viriliter stabilire conatus, hebræosq; compellers ad
sabbati observantiam divinorum cultum legaliumq;
exactam praxin glorioso fine initium Regni Dari-
nothi coronavit. Cum diu regnaffet, et sibi vitæ finem
adeffe suspicaretur, sibi convocatis Artaxerfe, et Cyro
filiis, huic magnâ quâdam præfecturâ affignatâ altern ad
regnum destinato, vitâ decessit.

▲ **Darius the Great**

Event: Expanding the Persian Empire.

Role: Darius the Great united the quarreling factions of Cyrus the Great's kingdom and expanded it east to India and west into Europe. His political skill helped unite people of different languages, religions, and ethnic origins.

the throne. An imposter named Gaumata came forward claiming he was Smerdis—son of Cyrus, the founder of Persia—and therefore entitled to rule the kingdom. Gaumata was only in power for about a year before the young and ambitious Darius and six of his friends decided to oust him from the throne. What followed is one of the strangest legends of ancient times.

According to the stories repeated by Herodotus and others, Darius and his friends surprised Gaumata in a fortress in the territory of the Medes and killed him. The seven allies then arranged to select the new king by a lottery: they would gather the next morning on horses, and the owner of the first horse to neigh would become king. One of Darius's stablehands learned of this plan and stationed a mare near the spot where Darius would ride up on his steed. The steed neighed, and Darius became king.

Reuniting Persia. Whether or not the legend is true, Darius did take the throne and was faced with immediate problems. Persia was divided into several provinces in which the conquered peoples were free to live much as they had before the Persian conquest. With the disturbing death of Cambyses and the short rule of Gaumata, these provinces had become restless. The people of Susa, Babylon, and Lydia were among the rebels who raised powerful armies of their own and threatened to withdraw from Persian rule. Darius spent his first years as king trying to avert rebellion in the provinces.

With a small army of loyal Persians and Medes, Darius began reconstructing the empire of Cyrus the Great by war and by diplomacy. He also partook of the time-honored tradition of marrying into the families of his potential opponents. Darius wed the wife of the late Otanes, one of the band who executed Gaumata. Then, to cement his claim to the title, he married two of Cyrus's daughters and one of his granddaughters. By 519 B.C. he had reunited the Persians.

Organizing Persia. Darius followed the example of Cyrus in organizing his government. He divided Persia into twenty provinces, each ruled fairly independently by a satrap, or regional governor. Although his own god was Ahura Mazda, Darius held

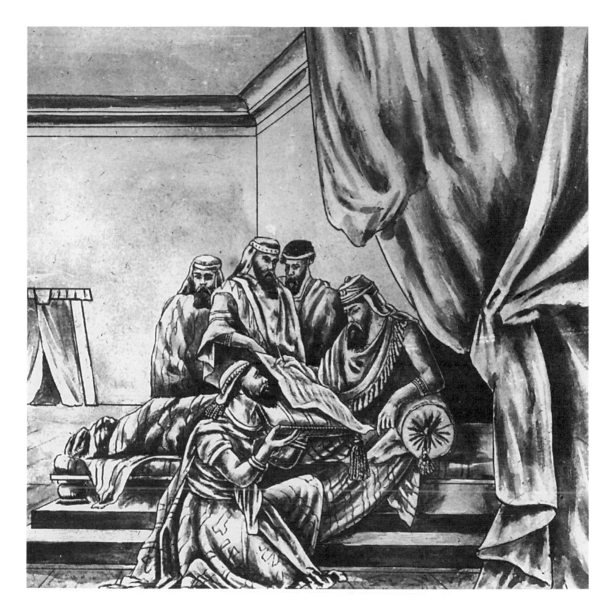

▲ Darius the Great signing the decree enabling the Hebrews to rebuild their temple; he believed that each conquered people should have the freedom to practice there own religion.

that each conquered people should have the freedom to practice their own religion and even helped complete the temple in Palestine that had been promised to the Hebrews by Cyrus. He also standardized the Persian monetary system and introduced a new gold coin that bore a picture of himself as an archer.

Darius's extension of trade took his ships from the Indus River in northwest India to the Nile in Africa, and as far west in the Mediterranean as Italy and the ancient North African town of Carthage. He also developed an efficient postal, trade, and communications route by land.

Participation: Expanding the Persian Empire

Into India. King Cyrus had expanded the Persian Empire eastward and westward. He had secured his gains by building towns along the kingdom's northern border to protect against invading tribes. Darius carried on this development, building towns south of the Hindu Kush, a southwest Asian mountain range. His explorers and armies marched into the area of the seven rivers called the Punjab, claimed that part of Pakistan and northwest India for Persia, and established a firm base of towns and trade routes.

Once situated in the Punjab, Darius assigned one of his most trusted and capable sailors to venture down the Indus River in search of a trade route to the Indian Ocean. This sailor, Scylax, reached the ocean and later explored the coast of Africa and the Nile River. Egypt was then ruled by Persia, and Darius was eager to use the Nile to find additional routes to the East.

> ### Darius Looks Back on His Reign
>
> Two centuries after Darius's death—just before Alexander the Great captured Persia—this statement was found beneath a carving of the throne of Persia: "If you now shall ask how many are the lands which Darius the King has seized, then look at those who bear this throne; then you shall know, then shall it be known to you: the spear of the Persians has gone forth far" (Fox, p. 105).

Building waterways. Scylax returned to Persia with accounts of his voyages to the Indian Ocean and Egypt. He advised Darius that a route east to rich sources in Africa and India could be established if the Nile River were connected to the

◀
The death of Darius the Great; his political skill helped unite people of different languages, religions, and ethnic groups.

▲ A cylinder seal, circa 500 B.C., and impression depicting Darius in his chariot hunting lions. He also introduced a gold coin that bore a picture of himself as an archer.

Red Sea. On his counsel, Darius ordered the construction of such a waterway. The canal allowed his trading ships to sail from Egypt through the Red Sea to Persia.

Westward expansion. The images of Darius at his grave site are most likely idealized, since he decided how his commissioned artists should make him look. The cliff sculptures show a tall, well-built man with a ruggedly handsome face covered by a square-cut beard, much like those worn by Egyptian pharaohs. He is seen sitting erect upon his throne—a throne borne on the backs of Greeks who appear to be submitting to the will of Persia. But in fact, only a few Greek cities of Ionia, located along the eastern Mediterranean coast, were ruled by Persia. The Persian view of Macedonia, a northern Greek state, seems to have been even more arrogant and inaccurate. (In Persia, Macedonians were called *yona takabara,* or "Greeks who wear their shields on their heads.")

Around 513 B.C. Darius felt it necessary to mount a war to push back the Scythians, a rising power that originated in the southwest Asian lands near the Caspian Sea and now threatened his northwestern border. He raised a great army that crossed from present-day Turkey into Europe to the mouth of the Danube, taking Thrace (north of Greece and east of Macedonia) for the empire. Darius had extended the Persian boundary westward but lost the final battle with the Scythians. He then retreated to Persia, leaving only one army behind to hold on to Thrace.

Aftermath

Ionia. The Greek cities of Ionia remained rebellious for the rest of the sixth century B.C. Seeking freedom, democracy, and an end to rule by appointed representatives of the Persian Empire, the Ionian cities banded together and revolted in 501 B.C. They were not strong enough to win alone, but Athens had agreed to help them in their quest for independence. It took considerable effort by Darius's armies to put down the revolution, and this left relations between Persia and Athens strained. Darius targeted Athens for his next conquest.

Defeats. With an army and navy stronger than those of his opponents and their neighbors, Darius felt confident that he could take the Athenians. Nevertheless, the Persian army met defeat at Mount Athos on the way to Athens in 492 B.C. Two years later they failed again at Marathon in their second battle with the Greeks.

Darius was determined to fight the Greeks for a third time. Before he could rebuild his attack force, however, a new rebellion broke out, this time in Egypt. The great king died at Naqsh-e Rostam in 486 B.C.

For More Information

Bamm, Peter. *Alexander the Great: Power as Destiny.* New York: McGraw-Hill, 1968.

Fox, Robin Lane. *Alexander the Great: A Biography.* New York: Dial, 1974.

Mercer, Charles. *Alexander the Great.* New York: American Heritage, 1962.

Silverberg, Robert. *To the Rock of Darius: The Story of Henry Rawlinson.* New York: Holt, Rinehart and Winston, 1966.

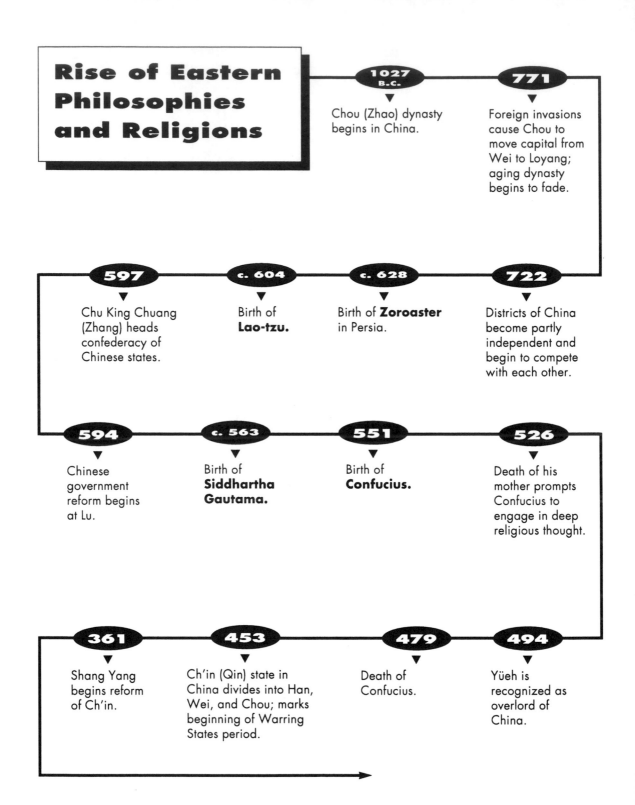

Rise of Eastern Philosophies and Religions

1027 B.C.
Chou (Zhao) dynasty begins in China.

771
Foreign invasions cause Chou to move capital from Wei to Loyang; aging dynasty begins to fade.

597
Chu King Chuang (Zhang) heads confederacy of Chinese states.

c. 604
Birth of **Lao-tzu.**

c. 628
Birth of **Zoroaster** in Persia.

722
Districts of China become partly independent and begin to compete with each other.

594
Chinese government reform begins at Lu.

c. 563
Birth of **Siddhartha Gautama.**

551
Birth of **Confucius.**

526
Death of his mother prompts Confucius to engage in deep religious thought.

361
Shang Yang begins reform of Ch'in.

453
Ch'in (Qin) state in China divides into Han, Wei, and Chou; marks beginning of Warring States period.

479
Death of Confucius.

494
Yüeh is recognized as overlord of China.

RISE OF EASTERN PHILOSOPHIES AND RELIGIONS

The period from 700 to 300 B.C. was one of reform in the Middle East and Asia. Babylon and Assyria were beginning to fade in the Middle East, while a new power, Persia, was growing into one of the greatest empires of the ancient world. The vast economic and social differences between the upper and lower classes encouraged reform in India, and the very old dynasty that had held China together in a feudal state began to break up. A loosely bound collection of seven powerful states in China was wracked by ongoing quarreling. By 453 B.C. the Chinese states were engaged in outright wars that would later be stifled by the rulers of the Ch'in (also spelled Qin) state and the emergence of another all-powerful dynasty.

Persia. Around the same time—in the fifth and sixth centuries B.C.—Pythagoras, Herodotus, and Socrates were reshaping Western thought (see **Rise of Western Philosophies**). A century before them, **Zoroaster,** a Persian priest, was developing a groundbreaking new idea about the basic goodness of human beings and their power to direct their own lives. His ideas grew into a new religion called Zoroastrianism, which was adopted by Persian leaders Cyrus the Great and Darius the Great. Some observers feel that these innovative religious ideals may have influenced how the two warrior-kings treated the people they conquered.

India. Hinduism had long been the dominant religious philosophy in India. Under Hinduism, the region was locked in a system of castes that separated people by social status, keeping some in constant poverty and isolation. The contrast between the lives of the very wealthy and the perpetually poor raised questions in the mind of **Siddhartha Gautama,** who gave up his princely life to help the downtrodden. His philosophy, much like that of Zoroaster, centered on treating others with respect. The ideas of Siddhartha later grew into the Buddhist religion. This new religion swept through India and then into other Asian states, raising a tremendous following. As a result, Hinduism was reformed and reborn in India.

China. The Chou (also spelled Zhao) dynasty that had controlled China since 1027 B.C. was growing old and corrupt. As early as the 700s B.C., the dynasty had broken into a collection of loosely allied states, and within 250 years these states would be at war with one another. The constant threat of invaders from the north only heightened the region's state of turmoil, and many Chinese scholars started to search for new codes by which to live. Thus began the age of the "hundred philosophies."

Philosophy reigns. Two Chinese philosophers, **Lao-tzu** (also spelled Laozi) and **Confucius,** stood out above the others. Lao-tzu is said to have abandoned his faith in government. He stressed the importance of basic human respect over man-made and religious laws as a guide to interpersonal conduct. Some Chinese philosophers, however, saw merit in the old feudal patterns of the first Chou rulers. In the old dynasty, they argued, people seemed content in knowing their exact position in society. This idea appealed to Confucius, who began to recreate the ancient writings in a collection that became known as the Nine Classics.

The philosophies of Zoroaster, Siddhartha Gautama, Lao-tzu, and Confucius reformed Persia, India, China, and their neighbors. The classic writings revived by Confucius were used for state examinations in China until the twentieth century A.D. Meanwhile, Zoroaster's followers were driven east by the growth of Islam. Their strongest presence is now in India. Buddhism remains the dominant religion throughout Asia, although it has been eclipsed by Hinduism in India. Taoism, the religion devel-

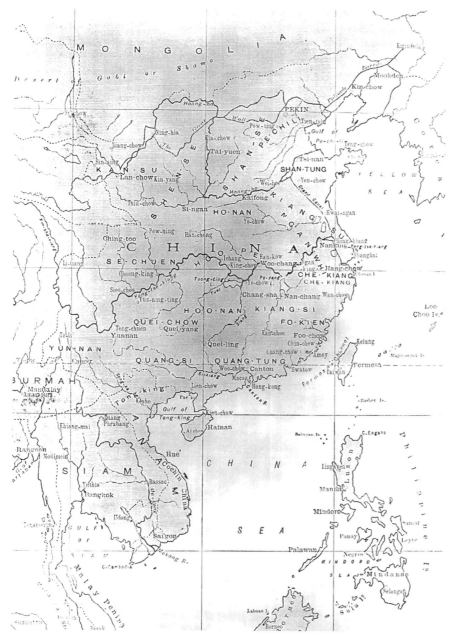

▲ **China and adjoining countries. The constant threat of invaders from the north only heightened the region's state of turmoil.**

oped from the teachings of Lao-tzu, now has its base in Taiwan and influences the world through one small book, the *Tao-te ching* (or *Daodejin*), translated as "The Path of Virtue."

Zoroaster

c. 628-c. 551 B.C.

Personal Background

The existence of Zoroaster (pronounced "zor o **as** ter" or "zor **oas** ter"), or Zarathushtra, as he is called in Persian literature, has been debated for centuries, but most historians believe that he was a real person. Still, little is known about his early life. The confusion begins with his birth.

Early life. Zoroaster is believed to have been born of noble ancestry, probably in a distant part of Persia known as Azerbaijan. A bright child, he received an extensive education and by age fifteen was prepared to devote his life to religious service as a priest. He may have become a member or even the head of an ancient order of priests called Magi, the dominant religious leaders throughout the Middle East.

For fifteen years Zoroaster studied religion and prepared to take his place among the wisest of Magi. Sometime in his religious life, he became a priest in a region called Raga, which some scholars place in modern-day Afghanistan. He also began to have heated quarrels over religion with an archenemy named Arjataspa.

When he was thirty, Zoroaster is said to have had his first of seven divine visions. The initial vision, he insisted, revealed a glimpse of heaven, a supreme god—Ahura Mazda, the "Wise Lord"—and various spiritual beings. Ten years later Zoroaster

▲ Zoroaster

Event: Introducing the idea of a single dominant god.

Role: Zoroaster was a Persian prophet who founded Zoroastrianism, the state religion of the Persians at the time of Cyrus the Great and Darius the Great. Zoroastrians worship a supreme god called Ahura Mazda and believe that the forces of good will ultimately triumph over the forces of evil.

▲ Illustration of the god Ahura Mazda as a winged disk guarded by two winged lions, based on a bas relief dating from about 490 B.C.

claimed that he had been put to the test by the spirit of evil, Ahriman.

Participation: Zoroastrianism

Following Ahura Mazda. Zoroaster's visions eventually revealed a new religion based on the concept of dualism, the idea that a constant battle exists between the forces of good and evil.

His philosophy centered on the notion that human beings possess the free choice to follow either Ahura Mazda, the god of good, or Ahriman, the force of evil. A person could help goodness to prevail by being pure in body and soul—by thinking good thoughts, speaking good words, and performing good deeds—and by seeing to it that the four basic elements—air, water, fire, and earth—remained pure. In this way, good would eventually triumph and all evil would be driven from the earth. The leader in this struggle against evil was the single, dominant god, Ahura Mazda, who was surrounded by lesser gods and seven important immortals, like archangels, who carried out his work.

Zoroaster preached that the earth's time to tolerate evil was limited to twelve thousand years. This he divided into four periods of three thousand years apiece. During the first three thousand years, the earth was in a spiritual state, not a physical one. Throughout the next two three-thousand-year periods, the physical world and its people were created, and the evil god began his effort to disorganize the world. These periods ended with the coming of Zoroaster. Following him, there would be a series of prophets and then, another three thousand years later, a day of reckoning. On this final day, Ahura Mazda would separate the followers of good from the followers of evil. Free will would dictate a person's final fate.

Around 600 B.C. Zoroaster took to the road to spread this new religion to the people of Persia (present-day Iran). Beginning in his own region, he succeeded in winning only a few followers. The first convert to Zoroastrianism was probably his cousin Maidhyamana. Legend has it that Zoroaster's early years of wanderings around Iran and surrounding areas—he is known to have visited the regions of Seistan and Turan—actually landed him in jail.

The Teachings of Zoroaster

The teachings of Zoroaster are difficult to follow. They place the burden of improving religious life squarely on each individual. For example, Zoroastrians are supposed to keep both body and soul *and* the four basic elements—air, water, fire, and earth—as pure as possible. It is therefore against religious rules to defile the soil by burying the dead. Consequently, Zoroastrians dispose of the dead by leaving the corpses to the buzzards and then discarding the bones without burial. Other rules are equally difficult to accept. Perhaps this difference and difficulty is the reason that for more than two years Zoroaster did not have much missionary success.

Writings. Zoroaster's religous teachings are contained in the *Gathas,* a set of poems he composed. All of his ideas about religion were eventually collected in a book of Scripture called the *Avesta.* The present-day holy book of those who follow the religion of Zoroaster, the *Avesta* was assembled from fragments of Zoroaster's teachings centuries after his death. It contains hymns and instructions on the worship of Ahura Mazda, the worship of lesser deities and saints, the process of making sacrifices, and the activities of priests.

The Deities of Zoroaster

Although Zoroaster taught that there is one supreme god, that god, Ahura Mazda, is surrounded by helpers. These helpers include the six subgods (earth, fire, water, metals, animals, and plants) and *yazatas*, or angels, such as Mithra, controller of light and truth, Apo, controller of the waters, and Atar, controller of fire. Also present is a god of evil encircled by hordes of demons, fiends, and evil spirits.

A national religion. Zoroastrianism eventually came to the attention of the King Vishtaspa and his wife, Queen Hutaosa, of eastern Persia. Both of them became converts, then the lords and ladies of the court followed suit. Soon Zoroastrianism was the official religion of eastern Persia. It was still the national religion a hundred years later, when kings Cyrus and Darius led Persia to its greatest heights. The religion's emphasis on the concepts of human decency, honor, and purity—so central to Zoroaster's religious philosophy—may explain Cyrus's reputation as a kindly ruler and conqueror.

Religious war. During Zoroaster's time, widespread religious disputes rocked Persia. Religious cults were constantly at war. In his old age, Zoroaster found himself caught in one such war between Iranians and Turanians. He is reported to have been slain in the battle by his enemy Arjataspa in Bactria, eastern Iran.

Aftermath

With the decline of Persia after the reigns of Cyrus, Darius, and Darius's son, Xerxes, Zoroastrianism also collapsed. It saw a brief revival when the Sassanids, a later group of rulers, took charge of Persia between A.D. 226 and 641, but then quickly faded as the Muslim religion overwhelmed the land. Today, only a small population in Iran known as the Gherbers and the Parsee people in India follow Zoroaster's teachings. Still, the idea of a single dominant god, people's free will, and a final judgment make Zoroaster's religion a true forerunner of the Muslim and Christian faiths.

For More Information

Latourette, Kenneth Scott. *A Short History of the Far East.* New York: Macmillan, 1964.

McKay, John P., Bennett D. Hill, and John Buckler. *A History of World Societies.* Volume 1: *To 1715.* 2nd edition. Boston: Houghton Mifflin, 1984.

Moss, Joyce, and George Wilson. *Peoples of the World: Asia.* Detroit, Michigan: Gale Research, 1993.

Siddhartha Gautama

c. 563-c. 483 B.C.

Personal Background

Early life. Sometime around 563 B.C. a child named Siddhartha was born to a royal family living in what is now Nepal at the base of the Himalayas, a huge central Asian mountain range. His father was King Shuddhodana, the head of the Gautama clan and ruler over the Shakya tribe of herders and farmers who inhabited the region's rich valleys. The king's palace was located in the city of Kapilavastu, not far from present-day Kohana, India, and due north of the ancient Hindu holy city of Benares (now Varanasi).

Siddhartha was the king's only son. Because his mother, Queen Mahamaya, died when he was just seven days old, he was raised and taught by an aunt, Prajapati Gautami. Stories about Siddhartha depict him as a solitary child who favored quiet play in his father's courtyard to typical boyhood games of war and sport. Still, Siddhartha grew to be a dashing young man well versed in the use of weapons. Legend has it that at the age of sixteen he won his bride by fighting other young men who wanted to marry her. He and the Princess Yashodhara lived in the luxury of the king's palace for thirteen years. In that time Yashodhara bore one son, Rahula, who was much loved by his father.

Abandoning palace life. Siddhartha became increasingly disenchanted with the plight of the poor who inhabited the streets of the capital city. After seriously contemplating the meaning of

▲ Siddhartha Gautama

Event: Bringing a religious revival to India.

Role: Struck by the contrasts between wealth and poverty in his own community, Siddhartha Gautama renounced his own royal position, became a beggar, and then developed a new religion. This religion, Buddhism, swept across India, giving hope to the lowest of the castes, and then grew to become a religious force in many other Asian countries.

life and the purpose of suffering in the world, he decided to devote the rest of his life to the pursuit of social change. In 533 B.C. he left his family and the wealth and leisure of the palace to search for knowledge.

Ancient tales of Siddhartha's departure indicate that he left the palace in the dead of night without bidding a painful goodbye to his son and wife. He headed for a nearby woods and then sent his horse and its elaborate harness back to the king with a message about his plan for the future. After trading clothes with an old beggar, Siddhartha went on his way penniless and without food.

The Birth of the Buddha

Various myths and legends surround Siddhartha's birth. One story tells of the queen's dream that she would have a son fathered by a strange white elephant. Her husband, the king, asked sixty-four Hindu priests to interpret the dream. They told him that the son, who was really his, would be ruler of the world if he stayed in the palace; if he left, however, he would become capable of rolling back all the clouds of sin and folly of the world.

Hindu experience. Siddhartha met up with a pair of Hindu priests who told him that he could only find the answers to his questions by giving up everything, even to the point of suffering great pain. Living a life of wealth had been an unfulfilling experience for him, so he quickly accepted the idea of having no wealth at all. For six years Siddhartha practiced the teachings of the priests: he fasted often, learned the difficult art of meditation (an exercise for emptying and opening the mind), practiced yoga, and studied the Hindu religion. According to legend, he adhered to this life of self-deprivation so completely that he nearly died of starvation and illness.

Understanding. After six years Siddhartha was no nearer the answers to his questions than before he left the palace. He broke with the Hindu priests and went off by himself to meditate. Shortly afterward, as he sat under an Indian fig tree, the answers to his questions about suffering became clear. Fighting off evil temptations from the devil Mara, Siddhartha finally reached a

◄

A seventeenth-century Tibetan silk wall decoration depicting the principal events of the Buddha's life. After seriously contemplating the meaning of life and the purpose of suffering in the world, Siddhartha decided to devote the rest of his life to the pursuit of social change.

state of perfect peace and understanding. He had become the "enlightened one," the Buddha. Through his vision of enlightenment, the Buddha learned that:

> Neither wealth nor poverty are the answer to human suffering; people need to exercise moderation in their thoughts and actions and follow a Middle Way that is always in tune with nature.

> For freedom from suffering, a person must understand four truths: All existence is suffering. Suffering arises from craving and desire. Stopping desire means the end of suffering. Stopping desire can be achieved only by following an Eightfold Path.

The Eightfold Path includes right views, right hopes, right speech, right conduct, right livelihood, right effort, right mindfulness, and right thinking.

Participation: The Founding of Buddhism

Some distance to the south of the Buddha's hometown lay the holy city of Benares, which housed more than one thousand temples and monuments to the Hindu gods. Here the Buddha began his teaching.

A religion for everyone. Twenty-five hundred years ago in India, the Buddhist religion was considered radical because it was open to all people. The two lower classes of Indians were not allowed to practice the Hindu religion, and others could only practice it under the complete domination of the ruling priests. But anyone could try to follow the Buddhists' Eightfold Path and earn that complete peace, understanding, and purity known as Nirvana.

The Buddha did not deny gods but taught that people should not rely on them to ease their suffering. Rather, each person should look inward for the strength to attain the Middle Way.

The conversion process. The Buddha converted five Hindu priests to his new religion and instructed them to spread his teachings around India. They immediately converted about sixty more people from Benares. Later the Buddha traveled with the priests to the city of Uruvela, where they gained one thousand more followers. He then set out for Rajagriha, where he converted

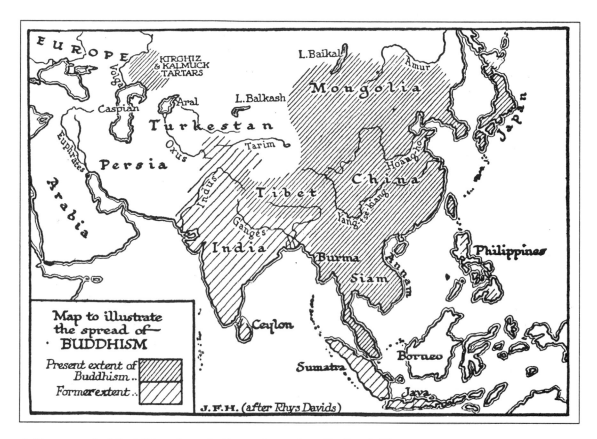

▲ The spread of Buddhism from India northeast into Thailand, Tibet, China, and Mongolia. Buddhism became a religous force in many Asian countries.

the king of the Magadha people. Back in his home city of Kapilavastu, he was able to convert his own son, Rahula.

For more than forty-five years, the Buddha and his priests—by now known far and wide by their distinctive yellow robes and wooden begging bowls—preached to the people of India's eastern Ganges Valley. The number of people who accepted Buddhism grew in the valley and spread throughout India, in many areas replacing the older Hinduism as the dominant religion.

Aftermath

The Buddha was still begging for food and teaching at the age of eighty when he died rather suddenly in a grove near Kushi-

▲ A twelfth- or thirteenth-century Cambodian Buddha made of stone.
Today more than three hundred million people are Buddhists.

nagara, a town on the Gandok River. The circumstances of his
death remain a mystery, although several writers have tried to
explain it. One ancient story holds that he was poisoned by a sus-
picious blacksmith. After his death, his followers continued to
teach the tenets of his new religion.

The spread of Buddhism continued through India and then into nations such as Sri Lanka, Nepal, Burma, and Thailand. In India, Buddhism served as a serious challenge to Hinduism and prompted a sweeping reform that forced the dominating Hindu priest caste to give way. Eventually, however, Hinduism was revived and Buddhism lost its power in India. By that time, though, the religion of the Buddha had taken hold in most of the other nations in mainland Asia. Today more than three hundred million people aim to follow the Eightfold Path of Buddhism to reach Nirvana, the state of no suffering.

For More Information

Latourette, Kenneth Scott. *A Short History of the Far East.* New York: Macmillan, 1964.

Mankind's Search for God. Brooklyn, New York: Watchtower, 1990.

Moss, Joyce, and George Wilson. *Peoples of the World: Asia.* Detroit, Michigan: Gale Research, 1993.

Seeger, Elizabeth. *The Pageant of Chinese History.* New York: David McKay Co., 1964.

Wallbank, T. Walter, Alastair M. Taylor, and Nels M. Bailkey. *Civilization: Past and Present.* 5th edition. Chicago: Scott, Foresman, 1965.

Lao-tzu

c. 604 B.C.-?

Personal Background

Early life. As with many ancient characters, the story of Lao-tzu (also spelled Laozi, Lao Tse, or Lao Tzi) was passed from generation to generation orally. The failure to establish firm dates of birth and death for him—estimates range from as early as 1000 to about 500 B.C. for his birth—along with the disturbing lack of any written history of his life led some scholars to doubt his very existence. Whether or not Lao-tzu was merely a mythical figure remains unknown, but many modern historians believe that he was in fact a real-life contemporary of—or perhaps a few or more decades older than—China's most celebrated philosopher, **Confucius** (see entry).

Lao-tzu, whose real name might have been Li Uhr or Li Ehr, is believed to have been born in Kihu-jin in the state of Chu, China. He was educated in the arts and became an archivist in the library of a king of the Chou (also spelled Zhao) dynasty. Sometime in his early adult life, he was able to travel through China to the border of India and observe the followers of the Hindu religion.

China in decay. By the sixth century B.C., China was in a state of political and social upheaval. The longest-standing monarchy in the world had begun to crumble under the decaying leadership of the Chou dynasty. As the central government broke down,

▲ Lao-tzu

Event: The growth of Asian philosophy.

Role: Influenced by the political disunity that rocked China in the sixth century B.C., Lao-tzu developed his own philosophy of how people should conduct their lives—a system that conflicted with the ideas of Confucius, Asia's most famous philosopher.

several smaller kingdoms began taking control of the region. The turmoil led scholars to develop various theories of reform. Li Uhr came to believe that most of the world's troubles resulted from human attempts to control or change nature. He pursued a career as an educator and focused on the study of down-to-earth reasoning as well as mystical thought. *Tao* (also spelled *Dao*), a Chinese word meaning "the path" or "the way," represented the total force of all of nature for Li Uhr, and he maintained that all people should strive to become a part of that force.

Confucius and Taoism. Li Uhr gained a reputation for his wisdom and his unusual ideas and, according to the tales of oral tradition, was visited by Confucius. While Confucius proposed that peace and contentment stemmed from the maintenance of political order and adherence to social laws, Li Uhr shunned man-made laws, wealth, and attempts at societal change, stressing instead the importance of humanity's complete communion with nature. He firmly believed that the natural way could not be altered; situations would change by themselves at the right and natural time. Li Uhr soon gathered a following of students, or disciples, who gave him a new name, Lao-tzu, meaning "old master" or "wise, old philosopher."

> ## Lao-tzu on Tao
>
> "There is a thing, formless yet complete. Before Heaven and Earth it existed. Without sound, without substance, it stands alone without changing.... One may think of it as the mother of all beneath Heaven. We do not know its name, but we term it *Tao*" (Lao-tzu in Wallbank, Taylor, and Bailkey, p. 83)

Participation: Taoism and the *Tao-te ching*

The quest for Tao. Lao-tzu taught the people of China that the gods had given every person free will—and that certain responsibilities came with that freedom. A person was obligated to be charitable, kind, and virtuous and strive for harmony with nature even in the face of rapid societal change. He felt it was

◄
A detail from the Chinese taoist freso *Lord of the Southern Dipper* featuring Lao-tzu. Lao-tzu's philosophy of how people should live their lives conflicted with the ideas of Confucius.

more important to seek an understanding of human beings and an earthly life than to be overly preoccupied with spirits, gods, and the afterlife. All human efforts, therefore, were to be directed toward knowing and becoming part of Tao.

The pursuit of Tao, according to Lao-tzu, was best aided by observing silence, solitude, passiveness, and humility. An ideal society, he preached, was a collection of villages so close that the citizens of one city could hear a clock in the next town, but no one hearing the sound would care to know who owned the clock. The citizens of such a society were said to follow *wu wei* (or *wowei*), doing everything by doing nothing.

The books of Tao. Before setting off for a period of solitude in the wilderness, Lao-tzu is believed to have written a book that brought the Taoist wisdom to all the world. The book, called the *Tao-te ching* (also spelled *Daodejin*), which has been translated as "The Path of Virtue," is easy to read and filled with short passages and old sayings.

Some Excerpts from the *Tao-te ching*

Tao invariably does nothing, and yet there is nothing that is not done.

Banish sageliness, discard wisdom, and the people will be benefited a hundred fold.

He who keeps his tenderness is called strong.

Weapons, even when they are victorious, are not blessed among tools.

Amass a store of gold and jade, and no one can protect it.

Better to stop short than fill to the brim.

Hold fast to quietude.

(Lao-tzu in Bahm, p. 17)

After completing the *Tao-te ching,* the ancient oral stories tell us, Lao-tzu wandered off into the wilderness, never to be seen again. A variety of myths have arisen to account for the philosopher's fate. One such story claims that he lived in solitude to be 160 years old.

Aftermath

From philosophy to religion. For many years in China, the followers of Tao were few in number. But as the society's old ways broke down and Buddhist ideas reached China from India, Taoism also became more acceptable. Monasteries began to appear in China, then Japan, Indochina, and throughout Asia. To make the Tao sect into an organized religion, a celestial master, a pope like character, was made head of the church.

Taoism and government. One central tenet of Taoism has had a lasting influence on governments worldwide: if things in nature are left alone, they will take care of themselves. In government this is referred to as the *laissez-faire* doctrine (meaning "leave alone to do")—a "hands off" approach to economic, commerce, and trade matters.

The philosophy of Taoism became a religion that has lasted for more than two thousand years. It maintains a strong following in the late twentieth century under a young celestial master who lives in Taiwan.

The Question of Gods

Lao-tzu never advocated godly worship. The Chinese people, however, found great comfort in devotion to the gods, so later Taoists incorporated them into the religion. Among them were Yu Huang, the Jade Emperor or head god; a group of holy men, ideal men, and models for humans called the Eight Immortals; and a series of lesser gods in charge of all the things people found around them—gods who guarded everything from entire cities to doors. Lao-tzu probably would have viewed any worship of these gods as a waste of time.

For More Information

Bahm, Archie J. *Tao Teh King by Lao-tzu.* New York: Frederick Unger, 1958.

de Bary, William Theodore, Wing-tsit Chan, and Burton Watson. *Sources of Chinese Tradition.* New York: Columbia University Press, 1961.

Pye, Lucian. *China: An Introduction.* 2nd edition. Boston: Little, Brown, 1972.

Seeger, Elizabeth. *The Pageant of Chinese History.* New York: David McKay Co., 1964.

Wallbank, T. Walter, Alastair M. Taylor, and Nels M. Bailkey. *Civilization: Past and Present.* 5th edition. Chicago: Scott, Foresman, 1965.

Confucius

551-479 B.C.

Personal Background

Early life. The early life of Confucius was marked by tragedy. He was born K'ung Ch'iu (also spelled Kong Jiu) in the city of Lu (modern Shantung) in 551 B.C. His father, K'ung Shü-liang Ho (or Kong Shuliang He), was a former soldier in the royal army who became chief manager of a small town in the Honan province of China. K'ung Shü-liang Ho died when Confucius was just three years old, leaving the young boy's mother, Chung-tsai (or Zhongzai), with little income or property. But despite economic disadvantage, Confucius grew to love books and learning and obtained a well-rounded education, largely through self-study. By the time he was fifteen years old, he had dedicated his life to learning.

Government work. Confucius's political career began when he was just seventeen; he was married two years later. The young politician quickly earned a name for himself as a local administrator, placed in charge of business at the town granaries and, later, on the town grazing lands. In 528 B.C., when he was thirty-three years old, his mother died. Adhering to the old ways of China, Confucius quit his job as a junior government official and spent the next twenty-seven months in mourning.

Confucius as teacher. Instead of pursuing government work when the period of mourning ended, Confucius began teach-

▲ Confucius

Event: Establishing the customs and traditions of China.

Role: Confucius lived during a period of political and social turbulence in China. Believing that the country could find order by returning to the ancient practices of the Chou dynasty, he began teaching and writing about the old customs. His revival of traditional ways spread over China and dominated thinking there through the twentieth century.

ing. He had no schoolroom and charged no fees for his service, but his methods were so popular that he soon had a considerable following of students.

Confucius was disturbed by the political fighting that divided his country. During the earlier years of the Chou (also spelled Zhao) dynasty (a period of reign by a single family that began nearly five hundred years before Confucius's birth), China was an extremely prosperous agricultural feudal state with a central ruling power. In this hierarchical form of government, all citizens had a fixed position in society; lesser rulers governed smaller parts of the nation and controlled the people in their territories. Confucius championed the feudal system, thinking a return to the form would help speed the renewal of peace and prosperity in China.

Confucius?

The real name of the great Chinese admirer of history was K'ung Ch'iu. Western writers changed it to Confucius, which is Latin for K'ung Fu-Tse (also spelled Kongfuzi), or "the Master K'ung."

The Chou capital and Lao-tzu. The duke of Chou invited Confucius to the ancient capital of the Chou dynasty to study there. While on this trip, he is believed to have visited the famous religious leader **Lao-tzu** (see entry), who was also preaching reform. The two leaders' philosophies were very different, however. Lao-tzu sought peace through a communion with nature. Confucius stressed the importance of tradition and focused on the ways in which people behaved toward one another. He did not think of himself as building anything new. Rather, he claimed to be a transmitter, not a creator, and a believer in and lover of antiquity.

Recorder of old ideas. The old order in China had once been set down in six ancient historical texts. As Chinese dynasties tried to impose their will on the people, the books were destroyed. Confucius felt compelled to recreate this old literature of China.

Participation: Nine Sacred Books

Confucius continued his career as a teacher while rewriting five of the six original historical books, including *Shu Ching* (also spelled *Shujing*), the book of history; *Shih Ching* (*Shijing*), a collection of ancient poems; *I Ching (Yijing)*, the book of "changes," which dealt with foretelling future events; *Li Ching (Liji)*, the book of rituals and etiquette; and *Ch'un Chiu (Chunqiu)*, the spring and autumn annals, a record of the Chinese state of Lu from 721 to 480 B.C.

Confucius did not concern himself with issues such as life after death or punishment for wrongdoing. Above all else, he sought harmony in family and society—a goal that could only be attained through the righteousness and self-sacrifice of all people. *Li,* the order of things, was the greatest principle of the ancient Chou dynasty and, therefore, Confucius's most important source of guidance. If everyone followed *li* as a model of conduct and personal relations, Confucius contended, "everything [would become] right in the family, the state, and the world" (Confucius in *Mankind's Search for God,* p. 180).

So powerful were the teachings of Confucius that students followed him on foot as he traveled from town to town preaching. Over the years the philosopher and his students wrote four more books explaining the meaning of the ancient ideas. Much later, these teachings would be revived in China and would dominate Chinese philosophy through the late twentieth century.

Confucius on Government

According to Confucius, ancient leaders who wished to demonstrate "illustrious virtue" throughout an entire kingdom were first obligated to put their own states in order. Wishing to put their states in order, they first had to regulate their families. Wishing to regulate their families, they needed to cultivate their persons and rectify their hearts. Wishing to rectify their hearts, they first sought to be sincere in their thoughts. Sincerity in thought required that they extend their knowledge to the utmost. Such extension of knowledge lay in the investigation of things. (Confucius in Legge, pp. 5 6)

Aftermath

Return to politics. Confucius's desire to change the way China was governed led him, at the age of fifty-two, to return to public service. He became magistrate of a small town, Cheng-tu (also spelled Zhengdu), near the city of Lu, and governed so successfully that he rose to become minister of works and, later, minister of justice. Although his reformist measures gained him great

popularity among the people of Lu, they also angered powerful officials in nearby communities. With his political enemies organizing against him, Confucius was forced out of office within three years.

Wandering. The great teacher then began a thirteen-year-long pilgrimage in search of government executives throughout China who would try his ideas on a state or national scale. His efforts were futile. Finally, when he was seventy years old, Confucius returned home. He died in 479 at the age of seventy-three.

Han dynasty. The ideas of Confucius and Lao-tzu stirred a great interest in the pursuit of wisdom in China. But the age of the "hundred philosophies" eventually passed. Over the next five hundred years, China was the scene of more political upheaval. The Ch'in (also spelled Qin) dynasty arose more than 250 years after the death of Confucius. As the new order was emerging, the Chinese emperor Li Huang Ti (or Li Huangdi) became worried that the growing philosophies threatened his hold on the nation. He ordered that all the classic writing—especially the books of Confucius—be destroyed.

Despite the emperor's best efforts to maintain his grip on the Chinese government, the Ch'in dynasty gave way to a new rule, the Han dynasty. Another great Chinese philosopher, Tung Chung-shu (or Dong Zhongshu), then proposed that Confucius's ideas on respect for government and order be adopted as the official philosophy of the nation. There was a scramble to recreate the old texts that Li Huang Ti had destroyed, and Confucianism remained to influence all China until recent years.

For More Information

Chai, Ch'u, and Winberg Chai. *Confucianism.* New York: Barron's Educational Series, 1973.

Legge, James. *The Four Books.* Culture Book Co., 1978.

McKay, John P., Bennett D. Hill, and John Buckler. *A History of World Societies.* Volume 1: *To 1715.* Boston: Houghton Mifflin, 1984.

Mankind's Search for God. Brooklyn, New York: Watchtower, 1990.

◀

Confucius did not concern himself with issues such as life after death or punishment for wrongdoing; instead, he sought harmony in family and society.

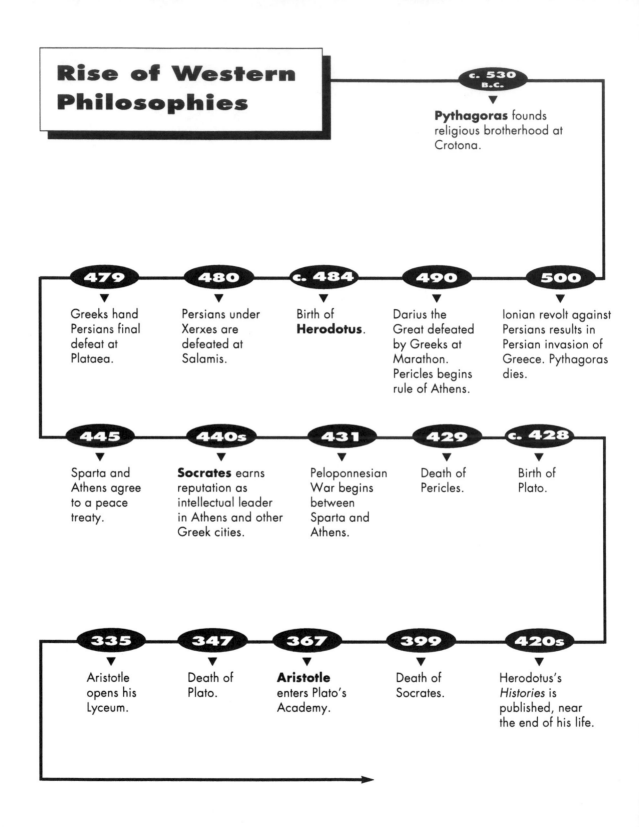

Rise of Western Philosophies

c. 530 B.C.
Pythagoras founds religious brotherhood at Crotona.

500
Ionian revolt against Persians results in Persian invasion of Greece. Pythagoras dies.

490
Darius the Great defeated by Greeks at Marathon. Pericles begins rule of Athens.

c. 484
Birth of **Herodotus**.

480
Persians under Xerxes are defeated at Salamis.

479
Greeks hand Persians final defeat at Plataea.

445
Sparta and Athens agree to a peace treaty.

440s
Socrates earns reputation as intellectual leader in Athens and other Greek cities.

431
Peloponnesian War begins between Sparta and Athens.

429
Death of Pericles.

c. 428
Birth of Plato.

420s
Herodotus's *Histories* is published, near the end of his life.

399
Death of Socrates.

367
Aristotle enters Plato's Academy.

347
Death of Plato.

335
Aristotle opens his Lyceum.

RISE OF WESTERN PHILOSOPHIES

Greece was one of the most advanced societies of the second millennium B.C. Between about 2000 and 1100 B.C., it flourished and developed refined pottery and metalworks. Then, around the time of the legendary battle between Sparta and Troy over the Spartan beauty Helen, Greek society began to decline into a "dark age." This period of decline lasted through 800 B.C., at which time city-states began to revive and grow, and trade routes were reestablished. The Greek way of life was beginning to be defined through a common religious philosophy, language, and set of interests.

Greek colonization. By about 550 B.C., Greece had ended a period of colonization in which politically independent Greek cities were founded from Italy and Sicily to North Africa and Ionia, the ancient name for the coastal parts of present-day Turkey. Sparta, on the Greek mainland, had emerged as a leading city, with an oligarchical political system (meaning "rule by the few"), but elsewhere new systems began to evolve. In Athens, democracy ("rule by the majority of the people") began with the reforms of Cleisthenes in the late sixth century B.C. Meanwhile, the wealthy and independent cities of Ionia became centers of learning. There, a curiosity about the natural world blossomed with the work of great thinkers such as Thales of Miletus, an early philosopher.

Ionia. Farther east a different sort of culture was taking shape in the rising power of Persia. Whereas the small Greek city-states enjoyed individual freedom, the Persian Empire fell under a central government ruled by one man, a "king of kings," as he was called. Persian power was consolidated under King Cyrus, who had conquered the Ionian cities by 540 B.C.

The Ionian Greeks rebelled against Persia four decades later, but their revolt was crushed by Cyrus's successor, Darius the Great. The Ionians had received some help from the Athenians and Eretrians on the island of Euboea, whom Darius then decided to punish. In 490 B.C. he sent an expedition across the Aegean Sea, but they met defeat at the hands of the Athenians and their neighbors, the Plataeans, in the battle of Marathon. Ten years later, a much larger expedition under Darius's son, Xerxes, was also defeated in a series of battles. It was the Greeks' finest hour, and the story of how they defeated the mighty Persian Empire was told by **Herodotus.** Thus Herodotus, the travel writer, wrote the first Western history book and is given credit for beginning the study of history.

Athens. Taking much of the credit for the victory against Persia, Athens emerged as a powerful rival to Sparta. Along with its political clout, Athens enjoyed cultural advancement under the leadership of Pericles. But the best-known Athenian was probably **Socrates,** the philosopher, whose concern for moral conduct was left to us in the writings of his student Plato.

It was one of Plato's own students, **Aristotle,** who preserved Greek philosophy for future generations. Writing on virtually every area of Greek thought, Aristotle put the Greeks' learning into the organized format that helped make it the basis of Western culture.

Greece and China. This period of intellectual achievement was not limited to Greece alone. Historians have noticed striking parallels in the political and cultural evolution of China and Europe from about 500 B.C. to A.D. 200. In both, a rise of many different philosophies accompanied a period of wars between states. Then a single powerful ruler took over with an empire that did not last long after his death. That empire was replaced by another one that drew its stability partly from the earlier philosophies. Finally, after several centuries, these empires collapsed under the combined threat of attractive new religions and powerful, warlike neighbors.

Parallels in philosophy. In addition to parallels in history, scholars have seen parallels among the teachings of Chinese and Greek philosophers. Confucius and Socrates both began traditions that later became dominant theories of the right way to live. Chinese sage Meng-tzu (also called Mencius) developed the ideas of Confucius, while Athenian philosopher Plato defined the moral concepts introduced by Socrates. In the fourth century B.C., Hsün-tzu and Aristotle played comparable roles in unifying the work of the earlier thinkers.

Pythagoras

c. 580-c. 500 B.C.

Personal Background

Sixth century B.C. Greek mathematician Pythagoras, like the later philosopher Socrates, did not leave any written records of his works to pass on to future generations. He apparently spent most of his life teaching and leading a community of followers. Because his biographies are based largely on legend, it is difficult to distinguish his original ideas from those of his followers. Several ancient writers, including Greek historian **Herodotus,** Greek philosopher and scientist **Aristotle** (see entries), and later authors such as Iamblichus and Porphyry, are among those who wrote extensively on the life of Pythagoras.

Oracle. Most sources agree on only the barest facts about Pythagoras. He was born in or around 580 B.C. on Samos, one of the largest and most powerful Greek islands at that time. His father was called Mnesarchus. One tradition says that Mnesarchus was an artisan, either a jeweler or an engraver. Another says that he was a merchant, which is perhaps more likely, since Pythagoras demonstrated a familiarity with ships and with the many trade routes around the eastern Mediterranean throughout his life.

According to Iamblichus, Pythagoras's birth was foretold by the oracle at Delphi (the priestess at the shrine of Apollo, who was to believed to be divinely inspired), who informed his mother,

▲ **Pythagoras**

Event: Introduction of mathematics into Greek science.

Role: Pythagoras discovered the mathematical basis of musical harmonies and formulated the famous "Pythagorean theorem" of right triangles. His teachings combined mystical and religious beliefs with mathematical and scientific ideas.

Pythia, that she would have a son by the god Apollo. In his teachings, Pythagoras always put Apollo first among the gods, and many legends draw a connection between the two. The story about the oracle is probably one such legend.

Samos. The island of Samos lies close to the coastline of what is now Turkey. Then called Ionia, the coast and its nearby islands had been settled centuries earlier by Greeks from across the Aegean Sea. Inland lay the wealthy non-Greek kingdoms of Lydia, Phrygia, and Caria. Like these kingdoms, Ionia's prosperous Greek cities would soon be taken over by the rising Persian Empire farther to the east. But during Pythagoras's childhood, the Ionians were thriving, trading busily with Egypt to the south, the inland kingdoms to the east, and other Greeks to the west.

Education. Historians speculate that Pythagoras received a basic Greek education, which might have included training in gymnastics, study of the epic poems of ninth-century B.C. Greek writer Homer, and lessons in playing the flute and the lyre (a stringed instrument like the guitar). As a teenager, he probably went with his father on trading voyages and learned some basic math to help with business records.

Participation: Introduction of Mathematics into Greek Science

Ionian philosophers. Pythagoras was born at a time of prosperity and intellectual excitement for Ionia. The island's proximity to ancient cultures farther east (especially Egypt and Babylon) sparked an interest in astronomy and mathematics, which seems to have led the Greeks of Ionia to wonder about the universe in a new way. Beginning with Thales of Miletus (c. 620-c. 550 B.C.), whom Aristotle called the first philosopher, Ionians up and down the coast developed the earliest scientific theories in the West. They speculated about matter, about the earth and other planets, and about the sun and stars.

Travels. The writings of Iamblichus and Porphyry, which date back to the 200s B.C., suggest that Pythagoras traveled to Egypt and Babylon when he was a young man, but there is no hard evidence that he made such a trip. Still, legend tells us that Pythagoras toured the wonders of the ancient civilization on the Nile: he is said to have gone to Heliopolis, which means "city of the sun," and the ancient Egyptian capital of Memphis, visiting the pyramids and the sphinx. He is also believed to have studied the Egyptian language, the ancient rituals of the Egyptian priests, and basic geometry, which the Egyptians used to measure off their fields after the Nile's yearly flood. The term "geometry," in fact, is Greek for "earth measurement."

Babylonian captivity. In 525 B.C. Persia conquered Egypt, adding it to the growing Persian Empire. Pythagoras's reputation for wisdom apparently impressed the Persians, and, according to his third-century biographers, he was taken as a prisoner to the city of Babylon by the Persian king. During his captivity, Pythagoras supposedly continued his studies, becoming a student of the "Magi," the famous Persian wise men. In addition to learning more about mathematics, he studied astrology and magic. (The word "magic" comes from the term "Magi.")

Brief return. Most sources agree that at some point Pythagoras left Samos forever. This may have occurred after his return from Babylon—but since not all scholars believe that he ever went to Babylon, the circumstances of his departure remain unclear. Modern students guess that he left Samos some time between 530 and 520 B.C. and headed for Italy, a place that forever after would be linked to his name.

Magna Graecia. As in Ionia, Greek cities had been established throughout southern Italy and the nearby island of Sicily during the period of Greek colonization, which spanned from about 750 to 550 B.C. These cities grew in wealth and power, leading the south of Italy and Sicily to be called Magna Graecia, or "Great Greece." Pythagoras immigrated to Magna Graecia, settling in the city of Crotona, on the sole of the "boot" of Italy. Crotona, a place much like Samos, had earned a distinguished reputation for its famous medical school, which might have attracted Pythagoras's scientific interest.

Pythagorean Order. When he arrived in Crotona, Pythagoras was well known in the Greek world for his learning and wis-

▲ A 1492 woodcut of Pythagoras researching the relation between pitch and tone and the size of strings of musical instruments.

dom but had not yet established himself as a spiritual leader and teacher. In Crotona he founded the Pythagorean Order, a monastery-like community of men and women working and living together under a set of strict rules and shared beliefs. Pythagoras is reported to have laid down a wide range of laws governing the daily lives of his followers.

Beliefs. Pythagoras's rules were based on his mystical ideas about the soul. He believed that each human being possessed a soul that came back over and over again in different bodies—sometimes plant or animal, sometimes human—depending on how pure it had remained in previous lives. His rules were designed to keep the soul from being polluted by practices thought to be harmful. Some modern scholars suggest that such beliefs came from the magical rites of non-Greek cultures like those of southern Russia; the early sources contend that Pythagoras himself possessed the magical powers of a shaman or tribal healer-magician.

Mathematics and the language of science. During Pythagoras's lifetime, the Greeks found a way of dealing with pure numbers by themselves, rather than thinking of numbers as merely standing for other things, like pieces of land. Pythagoras has been given credit for this discovery. Once numbers were freed from the purely physical realm and allowed to exist on their own, mathematical ideas could be applied to new areas of thought. Later, in the third century B.C., for example, a Greek scientist named Eratosthenes used geometry to calculate the earth's circumference and distance from the sun with great accuracy. Today, mathematics helps us understand many aspects of the world, from the orbits of the planets to the behavior of atoms. Mathematics, in fact, is the language of modern science. Thus we may trace much scientific achievement directly to the theories of Pythagoras.

Some Pythagorean Rules
1. Do not eat beans.
2. Do not pick up a fallen object.
3. Do not touch a white rooster.
4. Do not break bread.
5. Do not step over a crossbar.
6. Do not stir the fire with an iron tool.
7. Do not eat from a whole loaf of bread.

Music. Pythagoreans held that numbers lie behind everything—that mathematical ideas can be used to explain the world. A good example of this doctrine is the discovery of the relationship between numbers and music. Pythagoras is thought to be the first person to understand that music can be expressed in mathematical terms. If two tight strings of different lengths are plucked, for example, the difference between their lengths has a direct bearing on the sound of the notes each string will give off; it is therefore possible to predict what note will be produced by a string of any length before actually hearing it. Discoveries like this one led Pythagoras to conclude that all things have some kind of numerical basis.

"Harmony of the spheres." Pythagoras believed that the planets in the heavens created sounds of their own in their orbits around the sun. The sounds, he thought, were determined by the distances separating the planets, just as the length of a string dictates what sound it will make when plucked. This "harmony of the spheres [orbits]," taken up by later writers such as Plato, was an idea that lasted until the rise of modern science in the 1600s.

Religious figure. For Pythagoras, numbers exerted an unseen yet total control over the universe, and mathematics bore a very close connection to religion. Pythagoras was widely known as a mystic and religious leader, and ancient stories depicted him as almost supernatural in appearance. One popular legend circulated about his having a golden thigh, although this was probably an exaggerated account of a birthmark on his leg. Either way, the mark helped create an atmosphere of mystery around him. He wore pants—the way Persians did—not the usual Greek robe. He was also said to have sported a brightly colored cap or turban. His unusual dress and behavior clearly heightened people's belief in his magical powers.

Politics. Adhering to their pure and disciplined way of life, Pythagoras's followers became a powerful force in Crotona. With their support, Pythagoras soon took control of the city's government. He is believed to have introduced a system of coinage, as well as weights and measurements, into Crotona's marketplaces. (This was perhaps the earliest use of weights and measurements in the Greek world.)

Aftermath

Overthrow and death. For around twenty years, Pythagoras and his followers dominated politics in Crotona. Sometime around 500 B.C., however, a Crotonian named Cylon led a revolt against Pythagoras. Cylon and his followers captured and killed a number of Pythagoreans. Pythagoras himself was either exiled or escaped. He made his way to nearby Metapontum, where he later died.

Survival of the order. Cylon's revolt did not last long. Soon after the death of their leader, Pythagoras's followers were back in power in Crotona. Another revolt sometime around 450 B.C. led to the death of many Pythagoreans, however. Survivors—including Aristoxenus, who became a student of the Athenian philosopher Plato—fled to mainland Greece. Aristoxenus wrote about Pythagoras and his ideas, and Plato himself was influenced by them. These ideas continue to exert a profound effect on present-day philosophers and scientists.

For More Information

Burnet, John. *Early Greek Philosophy*. 4th edition. New York: Barnes & Noble, 1930.

Gorman, Peter. *Pythagoras: A Life*. Boston: Routledge & Kegan Paul, 1979.

Guthrie, W. K. C. *A History of Greek Philosophy*. Volume 1. Cambridge, England: Cambridge University Press, 1971.

Hussey, Edward. *The Presocratics*. New York: Scribner's, 1972.

Pythagorean Theorem

The rule that is known as the Pythagorean theorem states that in a right-angled triangle, the square of the hypotenuse is equal to the sum of the squares of the other two sides. The hypotenuse is the side opposite the right angle. The word is Greek and means "the cord stretching over against." (Burnet, p. 105)

Herodotus

c. 484-c. 425 B.C.

Personal Background

Suda. Herodotus was born to a well-known family in the Mediterranean city of Halicarnassus. His father and mother were named Lyxes and Dryo (or Rhoio), and he had a brother named Theodoros. Based on later events in his life, scholars guess he was born around 484 B.C. Aside from evidence in Herodotus's own *Histories,* the major source of information about his life is a tenth-century A.D. Greek encyclopedia called the *Suda.*

Ionia and its neighbors. Today Halicarnassus is called Bodrum, located on the Mediterranean coast of what is now Turkey (a republic that straddles Europe and Asia). Before Herodotus's time, Greek colonists founded many cities along Turkey's western coast, which they called Ionia. Farther inland lived non-Greek peoples like the Lydians and the Carians. Halicarnassus, opposite the large island of Rhodes on the southern coast, had both Greek and Carian inhabitants. Herodotus was probably of mixed Greek and Carian blood. His heritage might explain his interest in non-Greek peoples, "barbarians" as the Greeks called those who did not speak Greek. (Their speech sounded to Greek ears like the barking—"barbar"—of dogs.)

Xerxes' defeat. When Herodotus was a young boy, the entire Greek world was changed by the Grecian victory over the invading Persian army. Herodotus and other youngsters heard

▲ Herodotus

Event: Inventing written history.

Role: Called the "Father of History," Herodotus was the first writer to tell the story of an event in a way that explained how and why it took place. The events he wrote about in his *Histories* were the mighty Persian Empire's invasions of Greece in 490 and 480 B.C. and its remarkable defeat by the smaller, less unified Greek city-states.

tales of the great battles. Ionia had revolted against Persian rule, but the rebellion was crushed by the Persians at the sea battle of Lade in 494 B.C. Four years later, in revenge for their support of the Ionian revolution, the Persian king Darius decided to conquer cities in Greece as well.

Persian Wars

540s B.C.	Persian Empire expands under Cyrus the Great.
c. 500-494 B.C.	Cyrus's successor, Darius, crushes Ionian revolt.
490 B.C.	Darius sends first expedition to conquer Greece. Greek victory at Marathon.
480 B.C.	Darius's son Xerxes leads second invasion. Greek victory at Salamis.
479 B.C.	Greek victory at Plataea.
479-459 B.C.	Athenian power expands into an Aegean empire.

Yet, in 490 B.C., at the battle of Marathon near Athens, the Athenians and their neighbors, the Plataeans, defeated the Persian expedition. Then, ten years later, Darius's son Xerxes arrived with a much larger army to conquer the Greeks. A small Spartan force under King Leonidas tried to hold the Persians back at the narrow pass of Thermopylae, but they were cut down. Their sacrifice gave the other Greek soldiers time to prepare. Led by the Athenian navy, the Greeks won command of the sea with a naval victory off the island of Salamis. The following year, in 479 B.C., they won a major land battle at Plataea, badly defeating the much larger Persian army.

Expanding Greek power. With the Persians in retreat during the 470s and 460s B.C., the Greeks pressed their advantage. The years of Herodotus's boyhood and youth were years of expanding Greek power in the Mediterranean islands and in Ionia. The once-mighty Persians were now on the defensive, and Sparta and other Greek cities became fearful of Athenian expansion.

Participation: Inventing Written History

Trouble with a tyrant. According to the *Suda,* as a young man Herodotus was forced to move away from Halicarnassus "because of Lygdamis, the tyrant" (Evans, p. 2). Modern historians suspect that Herodotus and his uncle, a poet named Panyassis, tried to overthrow Lygdamis, the city's ruler, but failed. Panyassis was executed, and Herodotus was exiled to Samos, one of the largest of the Greek islands just off the coast of Turkey. Because his *Histories* contains an abundance of material on Samos and its colorful past, Herodotus probably stayed there for several years.

Wonders of Samos. On Samos, Herodotus learned about Polycrates, a tyrant who ruled the island sixty years earlier. Also during his stay, he saw the island's three famous works of engineering: a long tunnel cut through a mountain, a massive breakwater built to protect the main harbor, and the huge temple to the goddess Hera, the largest temple in all Greece. In the market, Herodotus saw the memorial to the Samian ships that had fought to the end as Persia crushed the Ionian fleet at the battle of Lade some three decades earlier. These monuments were reminders of the glorious past, of the marvelous deeds done by men who had lived before. And they all found their way into Herodotus's later writings.

A Trip around the World. At some point Herodotus came across a book called *A Trip around the World,* by a Greek named Hecataeus from the Ionian city of Miletus. Hecataeus had traveled in Asia and Egypt and then written an account of his journeys, which he published with a map. Historians today think that Herodotus read the book sometime in his twenties, maybe while in Samos,

Pronunciation Key
Darius: duh **rye** uss
Hecataeus: heck uh **tee** uss
Herodotus: huh **rah** duh tuss
Ionia: eye **oh** nee yah
Lygdamis: **lig** duh muss
Polycrates: puh **lick** ruh teez
Scythians: **sith** ee yuhnz
Thucydides: thoo **si** duh deez
Xerxes: **zerk** seez

and it was on Samos that he began taking notes, hoping to write a similar book. Herodotus then returned to Halicarnassus, according to the *Suda,* and helped overthrow Lygdamis. He was later forced to leave again, and it has been suggested that at this time he decided to become a travel writer like Hecataeus. His first stop seems to have been Egypt.

Egypt in the Histories. Herodotus's *Histories,* about six hundred pages in the English translation, is divided into nine parts, called "books." Most of the work is devoted to telling the story of how the Persian Empire rose and expanded, until it came in contact with the Greeks of Ionia and conquered them in about 540 B.C. The last three books tell how the Persians then invaded mainland Greece and met defeat.

But some parts of *The Histories* do not seem to follow a general, chronological plan, as though they had been written before the outline was final. The longest such part is Book II, entirely devoted to Egypt. In it, Herodotus describes in detail many of the country's features, such as the Nile River and the pyramids. He also writes about its animal life, the customs and beliefs of its people, and its long and colorful history.

Sources. In Egypt, traveling far up the Nile, Herodotus questioned people through interpreters. His best sources for information were priests, because they kept religious records. One part of Book II shows the lengths to which Herodotus was willing to go to obtain accurate information. Asking about the Egyptian god Hercules, whom he presumed was the same as the Greek god Heracles, he received a reply that countered the Greek belief that Heracles had not been worshipped for very long. He made two trips to get the right answer:

> To satisfy my wish to get the best information I possibly could on this subject, I made a voyage to Tyre in Phoenicia [modern Lebanon], because I had heard that there was a temple there ... dedicated to Heracles. I visited the temple, and ... in the course of conversation with the priests I asked how long ago the temple had been built, and found by their answer that they, too, did not share the Greek view [of Heracles' age].... I have also been to Thasos [a Greek island], where I found a temple of Heracles built by the Phoenicians [in ancient times]. The result of these researches is a plain proof that the worship of Heracles is very ancient. (Herodotus, p. 147)

A new interest takes shape. Herodotus visited many other places: the city of Cyrene in North Africa, ancient Babylon deep in

▶

Herodotus reading his *Histories* to the Greeks. Herodotus was the first writer to tell the story of an event in a way that explained how and why it happened.

the Persian Empire, the Black Sea and southern Russia, and the region north of Greece. Always, it seemed, he encountered Persia. Persia had conquered Babylon, Lydia and the other kingdoms of Asia Minor, and the Greek city-states of Ionia. Persia had also conquered Egypt and attacked the Scythians and Cimmerians of southern Russia before finally being thoroughly defeated by the Greeks.

Gradually the focus of Herodotus's studies began to change. While still interested in describing countryside and customs, he began to have a clearer idea of how he wanted to present the past. An idea took shape that would give unity to all of his writings and make the whole thing into one grand work with a single theme: he would tell the story of Persia's defeat by the Greeks.

Historia. On both the Persian and the Greek sides, there remained a few living soldiers who had taken part in the war, though the commanders were all dead. Their stories and memories, however, had been handed down orally. Victory had been, after all, the Greeks' most glorious moment, and Herodotus did his best to keep that success alive through his writings. "Herodotus of Halicarnassus, his *Researches,* are here set down to preserve the memory of the past by putting on record the astonishing achievements both of our own and of other peoples; and more particularly, to show how they came into conflict," reads the first line of his work (Herodotus, p. 41). The word translated as "researches" is the Greek *historia,* meaning "an inquiry." It is the word that others would also use to describe the type of writing that Herodotus invented—the word that has come into English as "history."

Herodotus and Athens. *The Histories,* probably published in the early 420s B.C., was written on scrolls of paper-like papyrus with pens made from sharpened, hollow reeds. It won Herodotus great fame. He gave public lectures in Athens, which was becoming the literary and intellectual capital of Greece under the leadership of Pericles. Indeed, he was a favorite of the Athenians, whom he credited in a well-known passage with saving Greece from the advancing Persians (Book VII, pp. 486-87).

Aftermath

Italy. The *Suda* records that Herodotus joined some Athenians who were founding a colony in southern Italy called Thurii. According to tradition, he died there around 425 B.C. and was buried in the public square.

Narrower path. Though *The Histories* was a "best-seller" from the start, later historians did not always have a high opinion of Herodotus's work. Thucydides, the second writer of history, chose the thirty-year Peloponnesian War between Athens and Sparta as his subject. He rejected the storytelling approach of Herodotus and aimed to be more scientific in his methods. Thucydides left out anything that was not directly connected to his subject, while Herodotus seemed to include anything he heard that seemed interesting, surprising, or controversial.

Archaeology. In recent years, Herodotus's reputation has been partly restored. Many archaeological discoveries have confirmed some of his theories and descriptions—descriptions that other writers of his time doubted, and even accused him of inventing. The best-known example is the famous Hanging Gardens of Babylon, one of the Seven Wonders of the Ancient World. When uncovered, the gardens proved to be exactly as Herodotus said they would be. Similarly, his accounts of peoples such as the Scythians were shown to be extremely accurate, even in terms of their religious practices and burial rites. (His reports of the Egyptians, however, seem to be less accurate.)

With his descriptions of everyday life, not only was Herodotus the father of history, but also the father of the more modern fields of anthropology and sociology.

For More Information

Boardman, John, and others. *The Oxford History of the Classical World: Greece and the Hellenistic World.* Oxford, England: Oxford University Press, 1986.

Burn, A. R. *Persia and the Greeks.* London: Duckworth, 1984.

Evans, J. A. S. *Herodotus.* Boston: Twayne, 1982.

Fornara, Charles W. *Herodotus: An Interpretative Essay.* Oxford, England: Oxford University Press, 1971.

Herodotus. *The Histories.* Translated by Aubrey de Sélincourt. Harmondsworth, England: Penguin, 1972.

Socrates

469-399 B.C.

Personal Background

Sources. Almost all we know about Socrates comes from the writings of his most famous student, a young Athenian aristocrat named Plato. Socrates apparently left no written record of his works. Instead, we see him as a character in Plato's dialogues, conversation-like writings in which Socrates discusses belief systems and moral concepts with his friends in a question-and-answer-type forum.

Ancient accounts of Socrates' early life tell us that his father, Sophroniscus, was a sculptor or stonecutter, and his mother, Phaenarete, was a skilled midwife (one who helps deliver babies). Scholars place his date of birth at 469 B.C. in Athens.

Athenian empire. Athens was booming during Socrates' youth. In the decades before he was born, the mighty Persian Empire invaded his homeland with a huge army and suffered a seemingly miraculous defeat by the weaker city-states of Greece. Athens had led the fight against the Persians and later, in the glory of victory, built a kingdom of its own called the Delian League. The league began as an alliance of independent city-states against Persia but grew into a virtual empire that made Athens richer and stronger than any of its allies. However, by the 440s B.C., Athens seemed to be alienating its allies by spending the bulk of the league's money on its own interests. For example,

▲ Socrates

Event: Measuring morality and exploring existence.

Role: Socrates redefined philosophy, separating astronomy, earth science, and the natural sciences from the larger examination of humanity's place in the universe and the way people should live.

the famous buildings on the Acropolis, the craggy hill in the middle of Athens, were built with the funds.

The fifth century B.C. was a golden age in Greece, when the leading figures in scholarship and literature flocked to Athens. Philosopher Anaxagoras taught there for thirty years; the first history book had been written, and its author, **Herodotus** (see entry), went to Athens to read his work out loud; plays by tragic dramatists such as Aeschylus and Sophocles glorified the city's mythic past and were performed at its official religious festivals.

Pericles. Behind it all was the leader of Athens, Pericles, a man of intelligence, boldness, and remarkable persuasive power. Pericles oversaw the expansion of Athenian might and coordinated the great building program on the Acropolis. Over a few decades, Pericles' Athens made more lasting and original contributions to world culture than any other community in a similar period of time.

Plato's Major Dialogues Featuring Socrates

Plato wrote more than thirty dialogues in all. Five of his early works are especially valuable for information on Socrates: *Symposium, Apology, Euthyphro, Crito,* and *Phaedo.*

Symposium: At a fancy dinner party, Socrates and others discuss the nature of love.

Apology: Socrates defends himself in court.

Euthyphro: Socrates and Euthyphro talk about religious duty.

Crito: Socrates, in jail, explains to Crito why he won't try to escape.

Phaedo: One of Socrates' followers tells the story of the philosopher's death.

Participation: Measuring Morality and Exploring Existence

"Marvelous to know the causes." Socrates spent most of his life pursuing knowledge. In the *Phaedo,* Plato has him tell a little about his studies: "When I was young," the philosopher reveals, "I had an extraordinary passion for that branch of learning which is called natural science; I thought it would be marvelous to know the causes for which each thing comes and ceases and continues to be" (Plato, p. 153).

Socrates had heard about the ideas of Anaxagoras, who believed that something called "mind" was the cause of all order in the universe. Socrates expected Anaxagoras to explain how "mind" created order—how it dictated, for example, the movements of the planets. When he read Anaxagoras's book on the idea, however, he was disappointed with the author's conclusions. While Anaxagoras claimed that "mind" was the cause of everything, he did not offer any reasonable explanations for his hypothesis. Socrates sought to understand the reasons *why* things were the way they were and spent his life searching for certain logical truths about knowledge and morality.

"Conscious of my ignorance." By the time he had reached his thirties, Socrates had gained the respect of many educated leaders, not only in Athens but in other Greek cities as well. Like them, he too had a group of followers who looked up to him. In fact, the oracle at Delphi (the priestess of Apollo's shrine at Delphi, who was believed to be divinely inspired) once proclaimed Socrates the wisest of all people. Socrates was surprised by the statement and argued that he himself possessed none of the answers he sought. He began questioning people known for their wisdom and reached some surprising conclusions:

> Well, I am certainly wiser than this man. It is only too likely that neither of us has any knowledge to boast of; but he thinks that he knows something which he does not know, whereas I am quite conscious of my ignorance. At any rate it seems that I am wiser than he is to this small extent, that I do not think that I know what I do not know. (Plato, p. 50)

Socrates finally concluded that the oracle had declared him the wisest of men because he understood that he was not wise.

Inventing the soul. The oracle's proclamation changed Socrates' life. Over the next three decades, he continued on his mission to find true wisdom and to expose those who only pretended to be wise. Through his studies, he determined that wisdom was the knowledge of how to live life the right way. Reaching that knowledge meant taking good care of the part of the self that distinguishes right from wrong. He believed that this part, which he called the *psyche,* or "soul," lived on after the body's death. The idea of the immortal soul became especially important when a new religion called Christianity sprang up over four hundred years after Socrates' death.

War with Sparta. Pericles' golden vision of Athens crumbled away over the last several decades of the fifth century B.C. The allies of Athens were bitter about their status in the empire during the postwar years, and various independent city-states grew fearful that they might be taken over next. Meanwhile, Sparta, the other leading city-state in ancient Greece, watched uneasily as Athenian power grew. Athenian forces fought several battles with Sparta and her allies in the 450s and 440s. The two sides signed a peace treaty in 445 B.C., but the nearly thirty-year-long Peloponnesian War broke out between them in 431 B.C.

Soldier. Socrates served as a hoplite, or soldier, in the Athenian army during the first part of the war with Sparta. Ancient pictorial representations show him squarely built with blunt features and protruding eyes. He was unusually strong and had a reputation for almost incredible bravery and toughness. On one northern winter campaign, he apparently amazed his comrades with his ability to ignore the cold, even on long nights spent sleeping in trenches. Back home, he is said to have walked around barefoot and worn only a simple light garment all through winter.

A new era. By the war's end, Athenian society had changed dramatically. Pericles himself had died in 429 B.C. during the terrible plague that struck Athens early in the war. His successors could not match him in leadership.

Sometime near the middle or end of the war, young Plato became a follower of Socrates. Plato hailed from an aristocratic Athenian family and helped support Socrates and his wife, Xanthippe. Socrates never took payment for his teaching. He thought of his followers as friends, not students; their long conversations were not lessons led by a teacher but intellectual searches they all embarked on together.

However, not everyone approved of these so-called searches. Socrates' pursuit of truth and knowledge left many well-known intellectuals looking foolish or conceited. By the end of the war,

▲ Socrates waited in this jail for a month before being executed, while his followers tried in vain to convince him to escape.

there were plenty of powerful figures in Athenian social and political circles who had grown tired of Socrates and his endless quest.

Trial. In 399 B.C., a few years after the end of the war, some of Socrates' enemies brought charges against him in court. They accused him of "introducing new and unfamiliar religious practices" and "corrupting the young" (Taylor, p. 106). The second charge stemmed from supposed acts of treason that had been committed by his followers against the Athenian state.

Most notable among those suspected of treason was Alcibiades, an Athenian general Socrates had protected after he was wounded in the battle against Sparta. A brilliant, stylish young aristocrat, Alcibiades was one of the most popular heroes in Athens, but he became embroiled in his own legal problems during the war. When his enemies brought charges against him in court, Alcibiades fled to Sparta. Afterward, his advice to Sparta

133

The Socratic Method

Socrates' method involved asking questions that exposed the faults in other people's arguments. In the following excerpt, he talks with Crito, who wants him to escape from jail:

Socrates: Ought one to fulfill all one's agreements, provided they are right, or break them?

Crito: One ought to fulfill them.

Socrates: Then consider the logical consequence. If we leave this place without first persuading the state to let us go, are we or are we not doing an injury [to the state]? Are we or are we not abiding by our just agreements [to obey the law]?

Crito: I cannot answer your question, Socrates; I am not clear in my mind. (Plato, pp. 88-89)

contributed to their defeat of the Athenians. Alcibiades had been one of Socrates' closest followers; Socrates' enemies tried to hold the philosopher responsible for the actions of his pupil.

Death sentence. Socrates defended himself at his trial in a speech that Plato later recounted in the *Apology.* In it, Socrates refuses to take the blame for the actions of his followers and states that it would be impossible for him to give up his way of life.

The jury found Socrates guilty on both counts against him by a very close margin. The prosecution demanded the death penalty, but the defendant was given the opportunity to suggest an alternative penalty, such as exile from Athens. Instead, Socrates asked for free food for life from the government: he had done Athens a favor, he claimed, and deserved a reward instead of punishment. By this time, the jury was incensed by his attitude and voted to enforce the death penalty.

Hemlock. Socrates waited in jail for a month before being executed, and his followers tried in vain to convince him to escape. Socrates refused, noting that he had lived his entire life in Athens and that he believed he ought to obey its laws. To run away would be to give up everything he stood for.

Many of Socrates' friends were there when the jailer arrived with the fateful cup of hemlock, the poison used for executions. As Plato related in his writings, Socrates asked if he could pour out a little of the drink as an offering to the gods, which was customary in ancient Greek society. The jailer refused, saying that the accused had to consume every drop himself. Socrates then drank the poison, walked around a bit, and waited for it to take effect. According to Plato, the philosopher's last request—directed toward his friend

Crito—was that a rooster be sacrificed to the god of medicine, since he had not been allowed to pour out an offering before drinking.

For More Information

Mason, Cora. *Socrates: The Man Who Dared to Ask.* Boston: Beacon Press, 1953.

Plato. *The Last Days of Socrates.* Translated by Hugh Tredennick. New York: Penguin, 1969.

Taylor, A. E. *Socrates: The Man and His Thought.* New York: Doubleday, 1952.

The Peloponnesian War

Between 431 and 404 B.C. Athens and its allied Greek city-states fought against Sparta and its allies over the Peloponnesian peninsula in southern Greece. Athens earned early successes at sea, but eventually Sparta, with its land superiority, won out. Athens was defeated, and the protective wall around the city destroyed. It was the beginning of the end of Athenian power.

Aristotle

384-322 B.C.

Personal Background

Aristotle was born in Stagira, a small town in northern Greece, in the summer of 384 B.C. Stagira, located on the three-pronged peninsula known as the Chalcidice, bordered the northern coast of the Aegean Sea. Even farther north lay the ancient city of Macedonia, a small kingdom that rose during Aristotle's lifetime to rule the entire Mediterranean world and beyond.

Doctor's son. Aristotle's father, Nicomachus, was the royal doctor for the Macedonian king, Amyntas. Young Aristotle is believed to have spent part of his childhood living with his father at the royal court in the Macedonian capital of Pella. As a doctor's son, he was probably trained in first aid techniques and basic drug therapy from an early age. This early training may have contributed to his love of science in general, and to his special interest in biology.

Plato's Academy. Aristotle's father died when he was ten, and from then on he was brought up by an older relative, Proxenus. At age seventeen he was sent to the most famous school in Greece, the Academy of the great philosopher Plato in Athens. Plato was more concerned with theories of morality and existence than with science. He sought to understand the nature of good and evil, attempted to define what was meant by concepts like "the soul," and contemplated the very existence of simple physical objects such as chairs and tables.

▲ **Aristotle**

Event: Determining the course of Western thought.

Role: One of the greatest thinkers of history, Greek philosopher and scientist Aristotle laid the foundation for centuries of Western thought. He was regarded as the single greatest authority in the fields of biology, geology, literature, politics, art, psychology, ethics, philosophy, and logic through the end of the Middle Ages.

Down to earth. Aristotle spent twenty years at the Academy, until Plato's death in 347 B.C. By that time, the younger philosopher was thirty-seven. With his balding head, small eyes, and skinny, bony legs, he was not a handsome man. He made up for it, however, by dressing well—his cloak and sandals were always of the best quality—and by wearing elegant jewelry.

Long before Plato's death, Aristotle had won recognition as the master's most brilliant student. His energetic gathering of research and his general love of books led Plato to nickname him "the reader." Gradually Aristotle shifted his interests from Platonic ideas to more concrete studies; he was determined to learn how the world actually worked and what made human beings, plants, animals, rocks, and other physical things unique. Instead of puzzling over the fact that they existed at all, he began to focus on their nature and function.

**From *Historia Animalium:*
Elephants**

"Elephants fight fiercely with one another, and stab at one another with their tusks; of two combatants the beaten one gets completely cowed, and dreads the sound of his conqueror's voice.... An elephant by pushing with his big tusks can batter down a wall, and will butt with his forehead at a palm until he brings it down, when he stamps on it and lays it in orderly fashion on the ground" (Aristotle, p. 640).

Rise of Macedonia. Amyntas's son, Philip II, became king of Macedonia in 359 B.C. Philip and Aristotle were about the same age and had probably known each other as children. A powerful leader, Philip quickly began a period of Macedonian expansion. Aside from improving the Macedonian army and capturing nearby Greek cities, he also attempted to increase the Greek influence on Macedonian culture.

Leaving Athens. Philip's growing power heightened tensions between Athens and Macedonia, and Aristotle's family connections to the Macedonian court may have caused him some problems around this time. When Plato died, Aristotle probably expected to replace him as head of the Academy. But that honor went to someone else, perhaps because of anti-Macedonian feelings in Athens.

▲ As one of the greatest thinkers of history, Aristotle laid the foundation for centuries of Western thought.

Aristotle left Athens soon after Plato's death in 347 B.C. He settled near a Greek city called Atarneus in northern Asia Minor (now Turkey). The city's ruler, Hermias, was an avid student of philosophy who had supported Plato's Academy. He invited Aristotle and some other Academy members to set up a similar school in nearby

139

Assos, where he provided them with everything they needed to pursue their studies. Aristotle later married Hermias's niece, Pythias, and the couple had two children, a daughter and a son.

It was in Assos that Aristotle finally stepped out of Plato's shadow and began the work that truly reflected his own interests. He observed animals in their natural environments and carefully recorded his findings. The result, a huge collection of notes and longer writings, is today called the *Historia Animalium,* or "Researches into Animals." It describes in great detail the bodies, habitats, and behavior of an astonishing variety of animals, from whales to woodpeckers and from insects to elephants.

Tutoring Alexander. Hermias was overthrown in 344 B.C., and Aristotle moved to the nearby island of Lesbos. There he continued his work on animals with the help of a young student named Theophrastus. While keeping up with biology, Aristotle also worked on other writings, including his famous *Politics,* about different systems of government.

Pronunciation Key

Aristotle: **ar** uh stah tull

Lyceum: lye **see** um

Macedonia: mass uh **doe** nee uh

Nicomachus: nih **coh** mah kuss

peripatetic: per uh puh **teh** tick

Soon after Aristotle moved to Lesbos, Philip asked him to return to Macedonia to oversee his son Alexander's education. Aristotle, now Greece's leading intellectual, was about forty-two years old; the future Alexander the Great was a boy of thirteen. Aristotle tutored Alexander for about three years.

Little is known about the relationship between the great philosopher and the future conqueror, but Aristotle's influence on Alexander does not seem to have been very strong. In *Politics,* Aristotle argues that monarchy—or absolute rule by a single person—is not an ideal form of government. He also expresses his disapproval of imperialism, a nation's policy of expanding by winning new territory. Yet, his young student, the son of a monarch, grew up to be a strong monarch himself. Alexander also went on to become one of history's great imperialists, conquering most of the known world and spreading Greek culture in the process.

▲ Aristotle and a pupil, Alexander the Great; little is known about the relationship between the great philosopher and the future conqueror.

The Lyceum. Around 339 B.C. Aristotle left Macedonia and returned to live at his family home in Stagira. Theophrastus and others went with him. By this time Aristotle's friends had become a group of followers whose studies and work he guided.

About four years later, in 335 B.C., Aristotle returned to Athens and opened his own school, one that rivaled Plato's Academy. Since it was located at the temple of Apollo the Lycian—Lycia was an area in Asia Minor associated with the god Apollo—the school was called the Lyceum. And because Aristotle often walked up and down a covered courtyard or *peripatos* while lecturing, he and his followers were referred to as "Peripatetics."

The students and other teachers followed the rules of Aristotle, ate their meals together, and once a month gathered for a symposium, a common meeting for dinner and discussion. At the same time, the philosopher continued writing what became a huge and wide-ranging body of work.

Collecting information. Aristotle first demonstrated his remarkable talent for observation and description with his *Historia Animalium.* As the head of the Lyceum, he expanded his research into the various branches of science, literature, philosophy, and history. For example, Aristotle had his students write essays about the political constitutions of 158 Greek city-states. The essays were then used by other students in their work and updated over the years. At the turn of the twentieth century, one of these essays, titled the *Constitution of the Athenians,* was found with a group of buried books preserved by the dry air of the Egyptian desert.

Aristotle's main goal at the Lyceum was collecting and classifying information, rather than focusing solely on abstract theories. Because of this emphasis on research, some modern scholars have called the Lyceum, not the Academy, the first true university.

Library and museum. Aristotle used his family wealth to start a library and a museum at the Lyceum. The library served as a model for those that were established in the period after his death; the museum specialized in the natural sciences. (Legend has it that Alexander—while conquering Persia and India—brought an assistant along to collect plant and animal specimens and send them back to the Lyceum.)

Avoiding Socrates' fate. In 323 B.C. Alexander the Great died, and anti-Macedonian feelings again swept through Athens. Aristotle left Athens, as he put it, "to save the Athenians from sinning a second time against philosophy" (Ferguson, p. 22). The first "sin" had been the execution in 399 B.C. of the philosopher **Socrates** (see entry), Plato's teacher and mentor. Aristotle went to family property at Chalcis, on the island of Euboea. There he died the following year at the age of sixty-two.

Aftermath

Unmatched influence. Until the end of the Middle Ages, the volume of Aristotle's writings combined with the force of his ideas—even when wrong—made him the most trusted and respected voice on virtually every scientific topic. Some of his theories, such as the belief that the earth is the center of the universe, were far from accurate. But for more than two thousand years, his pioneering work in biology has guided great scientists, including nineteenth-century British naturalist Charles Darwin, and his achievements continue to influence modern scientific theory.

For More Information

Aristotle. *The Basic Writings of Aristotle.* Edited by Richard McKeon. New York: Random House, 1941.

Barnes, Jonathan. *Aristotle.* New York: Oxford University Press, 1982.

Ferguson, John. *Aristotle.* New York: Twayne, 1972.

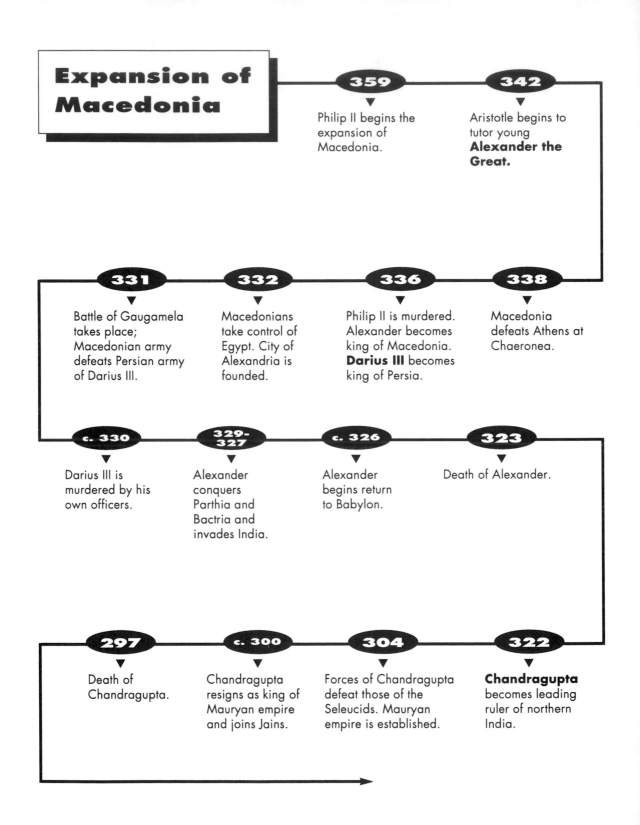

Expansion of Macedonia

359
Philip II begins the expansion of Macedonia.

342
Aristotle begins to tutor young **Alexander the Great.**

338
Macedonia defeats Athens at Chaeronea.

336
Philip II is murdered. Alexander becomes king of Macedonia. **Darius III** becomes king of Persia.

332
Macedonians take control of Egypt. City of Alexandria is founded.

331
Battle of Gaugamela takes place; Macedonian army defeats Persian army of Darius III.

c. 330
Darius III is murdered by his own officers.

329-327
Alexander conquers Parthia and Bactria and invades India.

c. 326
Alexander begins return to Babylon.

323
Death of Alexander.

322
Chandragupta becomes leading ruler of northern India.

304
Forces of Chandragupta defeat those of the Seleucids. Mauryan empire is established.

c. 300
Chandragupta resigns as king of Mauryan empire and joins Jains.

297
Death of Chandragupta.

EXPANSION OF MACEDONIA

The Greek world in the fourth century B.C. was in disarray. The alliances that had made Athens and then Sparta controllers of much of the region had disintegrated, leaving a number of small, bickering city-states. Into this disorder came one of the most powerful organizers of the ancient world—Philip II of Macedonia.

Macedonia, a kingdom in the far north of Greece, was viewed as a backward nation in comparison to the rich and sophisticated city of Athens and the disciplined city of Sparta farther south. Philip II, the king of Macedonia from 359 to 336 B.C., took advantage of the political turmoil that existed in Greece at the time. A skillful military leader, statesman, and negotiator, he forged ties with neighboring kingdoms in the south in a plan to unite all of Greece and then expand his kingdom into other regions to the east.

By 338 B.C. Philip II had built an army capable of challenging and defeating Athens. He gained control of all of the south of Greece, leaving only Sparta as a serious threat to his plan to claim all of the Greek states. Philip united the states he could control into a union called the League of Corinth, but in 336 B.C. he was murdered before he could complete his conquests.

Alexander the Great. Taking his place was his son, Alexander. While still in his twenties, Alexander gathered his lords and informed them that he would carry out the plans of his father, and he did so with great success. His army of thirty-five thousand battle-hardened soldiers marched into Egypt, conquered the city of Thebes, and completed their claim to the Nile River area by building a number of Greek-like cities. The largest of these was Alexandria. After the Macedonian army completed the union of the Greek states, it was prepared to move east toward the powerful kingdom of Persia.

Conquering Persia. The ruler of Persia, **Darius III,** was so confident in his power that he paid little attention to Alexander's conquests, even after the rebel king landed in the coastal cities of Ionia. Darius thought that his larger, better-prepared Persian army could easily defeat the barbaric Macedonians and their wild-tempered leader.

In 331 B.C. the two armies met at Issus, then finally in Persia at Gaugamela, east of the Tigris River. Although his army was greatly outnumbered, Alexander personally led the Macedonians to victory. From that time on, he was able to march through all of Persia with little opposition. With an army that had grown to about one hundred thousand soldiers, he captured the kingdoms of Parthia and Bactria and crossed into the Indus Valley. There he claimed authority over some of the small kingdoms in what is now Pakistan.

Alexander planned to move farther into India but was forced to turn homeward by about 326 B.C. He followed the Indus River south to the Arabian Sea and northwestward to finally arrive at Babylon. There the great king died at the age of thirty-three. The vast empire was almost immediately divided among his major generals.

The Seleucid and Mauryan empires. In the east, Seleucus, a Macedonian general under Alexander the Great, established another long-standing empire, the Seleucid empire. But **Chandragupta,** the king of one small Indian state, was simultaneously moving to unite most of India. Chandragupta followed the governing style of Alexander by dividing his conquered territory into individually governed districts. He succeeded in uniting the Indian kingdoms into the Mauryan empire,

▲ **Roman mosaic of the Battle of Issus; Alexander the Great is on horseback at left, Darius III is in the chariot at right.**

which stretched from present-day Afghanistan across India to the Himalayas.

Chandragupta's army fought and conquered the Seleucid army in 304 B.C. and won a treaty of alliance with the Persians. Having united much of India, Chandragupta resigned his kingship and became a devout follower of Jainism, a religion of nonviolence toward all living things. But just as Philip had prepared the way for Alexander, Chandragupta had prepared the way for his grandson, Asoka, to firmly unite an even greater empire.

Alexander the Great

356-323 B.C.

Personal Background

Alexander was born in July or August of 356 B.C., the oldest son of King Philip II of Macedonia and his wife, Olympias. Herself a princess, Olympias came from the royal house of the city of Epirus in modern Albania. Her family claimed descent from Achilles, the legendary warrior and hero of the Trojan War. Like most educated Greeks, Alexander probably grew up dreaming of the glory described in the *Iliad,* the epic about Achilles by the ancient Greek poet Homer.

Aristotle. When Alexander was thirteen, his father arranged for Aristotle, one of Greece's most influential philosophers and scientists, to travel to the Macedonian capital of Pella and take charge of Alexander's education. Aristotle specialized in the study of biology. On later military expeditions to far-off lands, Alexander is said to have collected and examined samples of local plants and animals, an interest most likely inspired by his famous teacher.

The murder of Philip II. By the time he was sixteen, Alexander was commanding troops in battle as part of his father's plan to gain control of Greece. In 336 B.C. Philip II was assassinated; a dagger was thrust into his heart by the captain of his own arsenal of bodyguards. Alexander became king of Macedonia before he turned twenty years old.

▲ **Alexander the Great**

Event: Expansion of Macedonian power.

Role: Inheriting the thriving northern Greek kingdom of Macedonia from his father, Philip II, Alexander the Great went on to conquer Persia and then continued east, crossing into India before his exhausted troops refused to go any farther.

Participation: Expansion of Macedonian Power

Philip II and Athens. One of the most able generals of the ancient world, Philip II had taken the seemingly insignificant and undeveloped border kingdom of Macedonia and made it into Greece's dominant power through a combination of military conquest and diplomatic skill. Two years before his death, a victory over Greek armies at the battle of Chaeronea had won him the title *hegemon*, or "leader," of the Greeks.

Pronunciation Key
Chaeronea: kye ruh **nee** uh
Darius: duh **rye** uss
Demosthenes: deh **moss** the neez
hegemon: **heh** geh mohn
Hephaestion: heh **phye** stee uhn
Macedonia: mass uh **doe** nee uh

Philip's staunchest enemies were the cities of Thebes and Athens. In Athens, a famous speaker named Demosthenes led the opposition with his "philippics," or speeches against Philip. On hearing of Philip's death, the cities celebrated, offering public sacrifices (feasts of roasted meat) and giving thanks for the assassin. Many prepared to revolt against Macedonia and the murdered king's young new successor.

Revolt. Regardless of the threats, Alexander and his army traveled south to Greece, and—without any armed confrontation or bloodshed—he managed to gain support from the Greek cities and acknowledgment as their *hegemon*. But this period of cooperation ended after Alexander turned north to put down a revolt among non-Greek tribes there. Rumors of his death in the fighting spread south to Greece, and Thebes and Athens immediately revolted.

In response, Alexander marched his troops down to Thebes, a trip of over three hundred miles that took thirteen days. The Thebans refused to surrender. After days of intense combat, Alexander conquered the city. Its people were either killed in the fighting or sold into slavery, the usual fate for prisoners of war. The king then tore the city down to the ground. Frightened by this display of Macedonian might, Athens and the other cities once again knuckled under.

Plans for Persia. Philip's assassination had come just as he was making plans to invade the Persian Empire, Greece's long-

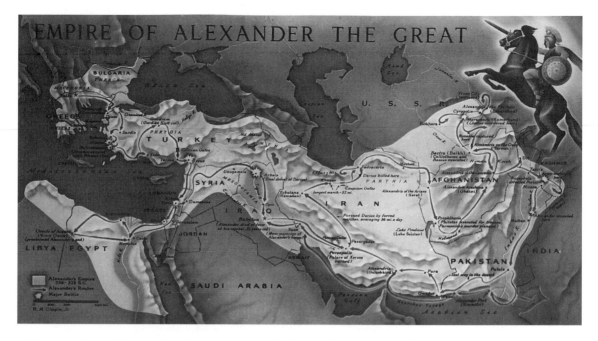

▲ The empire of Alexander the Great; though his empire broke up after his death, Alexander set an example of a warrior-king that others could only try to match.

time enemy. A century and a half earlier, under kings Darius and Xerxes, Persia had tried to conquer Greece but met with defeat. Philip wanted to exact revenge on Persia for this earlier invasion. With Greece under control, Alexander took up his father's ambitious plans.

Victory at Issus. In the spring of 334 B.C., Alexander led an army of about fifty thousand troops east into Asia Minor (present-day Turkey), which was then part of the Persian Empire. Along the coast lay many Greek cities under Persian control. After a year of fighting, Alexander won these cities back and then moved farther inland, capturing Gordium, where the ancient King Gordius had tied his chariot with the famous Gordian knot. Legend had it that whoever undid the tightly bound leather cords would rule the world. According to the story, Alexander simply slashed the knot in two with his sword. Shortly afterward, he defeated Persia's king, **Darius III** (see entry), in the battle of Issus in southeastern Asia Minor.

151

Phoenicia and Egypt. Though Alexander had taken Asia Minor from Persia, the rest of the empire, including Phoenicia, Egypt, and, far to the east, the city of Babylon, remained intact. Alexander's advisers never imagined that he would continue his quest for more Persian land.

Moving south, Alexander took the Phoenician city of Tyre after a long siege, then entered Egypt, where he met no resistance at all. In fact, the Egyptians granted him the title of "pharaoh," which had earlier passed to the Persian king when Persia conquered Egypt. The new pharaoh founded the city of Alexandria, which eventually grew into a well-populated economic and cultural center—and one of the most important cities in the Mediterranean.

Ruler and god. With the title of pharaoh came divinity for Alexander. He would be worshipped as a god because the Egyptians always considered their leaders to be gods. When Alexander made a trip to the shrine of Amon-Re, the chief god of the Egyptian capital of Thebes, the priest there addressed the new leader as "son of Amon" (Boardman, p. 311). Taken from Egyptian tradition, Alexander's role as both ruler and god would assume growing importance both in his own life and in his legacy to the Mediterranean world.

Final defeat of Darius III. From Egypt, Alexander and his men marched back north and then east, deep into the Persian territory of Mesopotamia (present-day Iraq). There in 331 B.C. they met Darius III in battle again, at a place called Gaugamela. Alexander was outnumbered but managed to defeat the Persian king for good. Darius III was later killed by one of his own generals. Alexander had done the unthinkable: the empire was his. As in Egypt, he took the title that came with victory. He was now Alexander the Great of Persia.

Eastern ways. For the next three years, Alexander was busy securing his rule over Persia. He put down revolts in Sogdiana, located in the eastern part of the empire, and married the beautiful daughter of a local chief. He also began to shun Greek tradition in favor of the ways and customs of the Persians. The most striking example of this new behavior was demanding that those who appeared before him crouch down to the ground—a submissive gesture that Persian kings had always required. This new practice clashed with the Greek ideas of equality and democracy, and many of the Greeks and Macedonians on Alexander's staff opposed it vehemently. The issue gave rise to bad feelings, especially after the strongest objector, Callisthenes (Aristotle's nephew), was executed on a charge of conspiracy.

Exploration and conquest. In 327 B.C. Alexander continued his path of conquest, crossing into India through the rugged Khyber Pass in the Himalaya mountains. For the Greeks, this territory was beyond the edge of the known world. After defeating the army of the Indian king Porus, Alexander's exhausted troops refused to go any farther. Instead of pressing eastward through India as Alexander had planned, they turned south and followed the Indus River to the Arabian Sea.

> ### The Charm of the Conqueror
>
> When Darius III fled from the field during the battle of Issus, Alexander captured several members of the royal family, among them Darius's mother, Queen Sisygambis. The queen was a strong-willed woman who took a liking to the young Macedonian king. The pair apparently became friends.

On the way, Alexander and his troops faced some of their toughest battles against the Indian warriors of the Punjab region, which is located in what is now Pakistan. In one such battle, Alexander was badly wounded while showing his usual disregard for physical danger. Finding himself inside the fortified walls of an Indian city under siege, he stood fast against everything his opponents could hurl at him. Alexander took an arrow through the chest before the Macedonians finally broke down a gate and stormed through to save him. Word spread that he had died, and in fact it took him months to recover.

Return to Persia. Alexander and his troops then embarked on the long and dangerous journey back to Persia through the coastal deserts of present-day Pakistan. Many in the army fell victim to thirst and disease. On arriving at Babylon sometime during the winter of 325 B.C., the king found that his long absence—and the rumors of his death—had weakened his control over the government. He executed or replaced many of the people he had left in charge. That spring, he ordered his Macedonian nobles to marry Persian women, and he himself took a second wife, a Persian noble-

woman. His soldiers were also encouraged to marry Persians. Alexander wished to establish a mixed society in which the Persian and Greek ways might exist together.

Aftermath

Death in Babylon. In the fall of 324 B.C., Alexander's best friend and chief adviser, Hephaestion, died. The two had been companions since boyhood, and the loss devastated Alexander. Grieving and still weak from the wound he obtained in the battle in India, he lost his own will to live. The following spring, while in Babylon preparing for an invasion of Arabia, Alexander fell ill with fever. A week later, he became comatose and died. He was only thirty-three years old.

Legendary figure. Wherever he had been—from Egypt to India—Alexander inspired legends that lasted for centuries. Later rulers, especially the Roman emperors, viewed him as a model of absolute power. Though Alexander's empire broke up after his death, he set an example of a warrior-king that others could only try to match in later centuries.

Following a Leader

Alexander inspired remarkable loyalty from his soldiers by suffering all the hardships they suffered, as his leadership in the Asian desert shows:

"Alexander, like everyone else, was tormented by thirst, but he was nonetheless marching on foot at the head of his men.... As they toiled on, a party of light infantry which had gone off looking for water found some—just a wretched little trickle collected in a shallow gully. They ... hurried back ... and gave it to him. Alexander, with a word of thanks for the gift ... and, in full view of his troops, poured the water on the ground. So extraordinary was the effect of this action that the water wasted by Alexander was as good as a drink for every man" (Arrian, p. 339).

For More Information

Arrian. *The Campaigns of Alexander.* London: Penguin, 1976.

Boardman, John, and others. *Greece and the Hellenistic World.* New York: Oxford University Press, 1986.

Lane Fox, Robin. *Alexander the Great.* London: Penguin, 1986.

Plutarch. *The Age of Alexander.* London: Penguin, 1973.

◄

Alexander the Great in Egypt; wherever he traveled, Alexander inspired legends that lasted for centuries.

Darius III

c. 381-330 B.C.

Personal Background

Darius III, originally known as Codoman, was born into a side branch of Persia's ruling family, the Achaemenids, who traced their ancestry back to a king named Achaemenes. Persia was part of the Median empire, and Persia's kings owed their obedience to the Median rulers until about 550 B.C., when Cyrus the Great overthrew the Medes and gained control of their empire. He and his Achaemenid successors expanded Persian power, taking over Babylon, Egypt, and Asia Minor (present-day Turkey).

Empire in decline. Defeated in its attempts to win control of Greece under Darius I and Xerxes, the once-glorious Persian Empire had been on the defensive for a century by the time Codoman was born into the royal family. His parents, Arsames and Sisygambis, were brother and sister, as was customary in the Achaemenid royal house. His grandfather Otanes was the younger brother of Artaxerxes II, who ruled from 404 to 359 B.C.

Times had changed by the time Codoman had reached his twenties. His grandfather's two successors, Artaxerxes III and Arses, were not the real powers behind the throne. Both were controlled by a man named Bagoas, the powerful and ruthless satrap, or territorial governor, of Egypt.

Poison. Bagoas poisoned both kings when he thought they were becoming too independent. With the death of Arses in 336

▲ Darius III

Event: Defeat of Persia.

Role: Darius III, king of Persia from 336 to 330 B.C., was twice defeated by Macedonian ruler Alexander the Great in battle. The second defeat, at Gaugamela in 331 B.C., brought Alexander control of the Persian Empire. Darius was killed soon after by one of his own officers.

B.C., the corrupt satrap needed someone on the throne who would follow his orders. He chose Codoman, a governor of Armenia who by that time was in his forties. Codoman had gained a reputation for bravery by accepting—and ultimately winning—a challenge to fight a warrior whose tribe was rebelling against Persian rule.

Installed by Bagoas, the new king took the name Darius III. However, to Bagoas's surprise, he had no intention of being controlled by anyone. Ancient historic records indicate that when Bagoas tried to kill him with poison, Darius forced the satrap to consume the tainted drink himself.

Participation: Defeat of Persia

Challenge from Macedonia. Darius III became king of Persia in 336 B.C., the same year that **Alexander the Great** (see entry) ascended to the throne of Macedonia. Darius knew that Alexander's father, Philip II, had planned an invasion of the Persian Empire's western provinces in Asia Minor. There, along the coast of what is now Turkey, many Greek cities had long been under Persian control. To liberate them from Persian rule—and to pay Persia back for its earlier invasions of Greece—Philip had called for a Hellenic campaign against Persia. ("Hellenic" is another word for Greek.) Philip's campaign for freedom was viewed as particularly ironic by the Greeks, since the Macedonian conquest of the area a few years earlier had stripped them of their independence.

Philip was murdered in 336 B.C., and the kingdom passed to his young son Alexander. It soon became clear that Alexander would carry on his father's plans for invading Asia Minor. But Darius paid little attention to the seemingly small problem of Macedonia. Persia, still a huge and mighty empire, had a strong, well-trained navy that controlled the sea and an army many times larger than the Macedonian forces. Darius never anticipated the extent of Alexander's military genius.

Invasion. Instead, Darius was preoccupied with the daily business of the empire, a small military skirmish in Egypt, and the traditional planning and building of his royal tomb in the capital city of Persepolis. Part of his foreign policy, however, involved providing financial assistance to cities such as Athens and Sparta, which were leading the Greek resistance movement against Macedonian rule. Still, Alexander and his disciplined troops kept a firm grip on Greece, even as he led an army of fifty thousand into Asia Minor in the spring of 334 B.C.

Darius's Greeks. The Macedonian conquest of Greece had created a huge number of exiles from the Greek cities. As a result, Darius had more Greeks fighting for him than Alexander did—a full fifty thousand Greek mercenaries (soldiers for hire) compared with only seven thousand in the Macedonian army. Trusted with important roles in battle, the Greeks remained loyal to Darius to the end.

Battle of the Granicus. Darius left the defense of Asia Minor to his satrap and generals there rather than taking command himself. One of the generals, a Greek named Memnon, commanded the mercenaries. He advised the other generals to destroy all crops in Alexander's path, to remove all valuables, and even to burn down villages and towns if necessary. Then, when the Macedonians were forced to withdraw out of hunger, the Persians could pursue them back into Greece. Failing to comprehend the full threat of the Macedonian army, though, the Persian generals refused.

The mighty Persian army met Alexander's smaller force at the Granicus River soon after Alexander crossed into Asia Minor. Determined to reach and kill him early in the confrontation, the overly confident Persian generals did not take the time to plan out the positions of their troops carefully. The Macedonians were then able to break through the Persian lines. Amid heavy casualties, the Persians fled.

March to Asia Minor. Within a year Alexander had won control of Asia Minor's coastal cities. Darius, realizing he had not taken the Macedonians seriously enough, attempted to win back the lost territory. He offered a reward of 1,000 talents of silver to anyone who killed Alexander. (A "talent" was an ancient unit of value; 1,000 of them was a large fortune.) He also put Memnon in charge of the Persian forces in Asia Minor, ordering him to carry

out the plan he had suggested earlier. But Memnon became ill and died before he could reorganize the Persian offensive.

Darius had lost his best general. Changing his plan completely, he decided to lead the Persian forces into battle himself—to confront Alexander before any additional territory could be lost. He gathered a large army and set out for Asia Minor from Babylon. There, seven hundred miles away, Alexander waited.

Alexander had been moving south through a pass in the Taurus Mountains now known as the Cilician Gates while Darius marched west and then north. The two armies apparently drew nearer to each other, but neither one had a clear idea of the other's exact location. They ended up slipping past each other, separated by only a few miles. It was Darius who first realized what had happened. Cutting toward the Mediterranean coast of Syria and then south, Darius brought his army up behind Alexander's. In an amazing stroke of luck, he was able to cut off Alexander's supply lines and gain a strong position to attack from the rear.

Battle of Issus. But Alexander turned the tables on Darius by marching his exhausted army back up the coast to a narrow strip of land. There, Darius's larger force would be less effective than on the wide plain; and there, just south of the town of Issus, the two armies slowly drew closer for battle.

According to various accounts of the battle of Issus, the Macedonians drove through the center of the Persian line in a magnificent charge. With Alexander in the lead, the soldiers struggled to fight their way through the determined Persian royal guard, who protected Darius in his chariot. Led by Darius's brother Oxasthres, the Persians fought valiantly but were slowly forced back. The horses of Darius's chariot went out of control, and Darius apparently leaped into a smaller chariot. In danger of capture or death, he lost his nerve. The king of Persia turned and fled for his life.

◄

Fighting around Darius III's chariot at Issus; in danger of capture or death during the battle, Darius fled for his life.

Pursuit. As they watched Darius run, the Persians lost heart. Many are said to have run themselves, trampling the reserve soldiers behind them. The Macedonians rolled over the fleeing troops like a wave, killing hundreds. With Alexander in hot pursuit, Darius abandoned the chariot altogether, leaving all his weapons and his royal cape behind and continuing on horseback. Alexander reportedly chased him twenty-five miles before giving up. Returning to the abandoned camp, he claimed the treasures he found in the Persian king's tents and captured several members of the royal family, including Darius's mother, wife, and children.

Peace offering. Darius fled back to Babylon and later sent his ambassadors to Alexander with a message: he promised to pay a large ransom for his family and offered Alexander all of Asia Minor in return for peace. It was a generous offer, and although Alexander's advisers urged him to accept it, he chose instead to send back an insulting message addressed from "King Alexander to Darius," not even giving Darius the courtesy of his royal title:

> In the future let any communication you wish to make with me be addressed to the King of all Asia. Do not write to me as an equal. Everything you possess is now mine; so, if you should want anything, let me know in the proper terms, or I shall take steps to deal with you as a criminal. If, on the other hand, you wish to dispute the throne, stand and fight for it and do not run away. Wherever you may hide yourself, be sure I shall seek you out. (From Alexander's message to Darius, in Green, p. 241)

For two years, Darius prepared for Alexander's next attack. Meanwhile, Alexander moved south, taking over control of Syria and Egypt. Finally, in 331 B.C., he marched east toward Babylon—and the heart of the Persian Empire.

Battle of Gaugamela. In preparation for his second meeting with Alexander, Darius built a new army composed almost entirely of cavalry (armed soldiers on horseback) rather than foot soldiers. And this time the battlefield—located north of Babylon at Gaugamela—was a broad plain instead of a narrow strip. Darius was able to spread his army out in a long line that threatened to surround Alexander completely. But Alexander once more showed his genius for military strategy, coming up with a plan that other outnumbered commanders—including early nineteenth-century French emperor Napoleon Bonaparte—would copy in the future. He angled his line back in a U-shape, drawing the Persians to the sides, and once again punched hard at the middle of the Persian line. The Persian guard fell back in furious fighting, and, as before, Darius lost his nerve and fled. The scenes of disorganized Persian retreat were repeated, but this time it was clear that Darius had lost everything. The empire was Alexander's.

Aftermath

Death in chains. By 330 B.C. Darius was preparing to surrender to his conqueror when he was overthrown by a man named Bessus, one of his own officers. Bessus put Darius in chains, declared himself king, and then—as Alexander closed in—had Darius stabbed. Leaving Darius behind in the royal wagon, he fled with his men. By the time Alexander reached the scene, Darius was already dead.

For More Information

Arrian. *The Campaigns of Alexander.* London: Penguin, 1976.

Green, Peter. *Alexander of Macedon, 356-323 B.C.* Berkeley: University of California Press, 1991.

Lane Fox, Robin. *Alexander the Great.* London: Penguin, 1986.

Lipsius, Frank. *Alexander the Great.* New York: Saturday Review Press, 1974.

Plutarch. *The Age of Alexander.* London: Penguin, 1973.

Chandragupta

c. 345-c. 297 B.C.

Personal Background

According to legend, Chandragupta (also spelled Candragupta) Maurya was the son of a local king in the eastern Indian region of Magadha, near present-day Bangladesh. The king was killed in battle before his son was born, and Chandragupta's mother went into hiding for the duration of her pregnancy to ensure protection from her husband's enemies. After his birth, the child's uncles arranged for him to be raised by a poor farmer, who in turn sold him to a hunter. The hunter used Chandragupta to take care of his cattle, and the boy grew up with no knowledge of his royal heritage.

Playing king. The ancient story of Chandragupta suggests that the young prince was destined to lead his people. When he was about eight or nine years old, Chandragupta invented a game that he played in the village square with his boyhood friends. Having declared himself king and his friends the subjects of the king, he set up a mock court in which cases were tried before him. A wise man named Chanakya (also known as Kautilya), who was visiting the village, observed Chandragupta at play. Impressed by the boy's kingly behavior, Chanakya gave his hunter-guardian a large amount of money and then took Chandragupta back to his own city of Taxila.

▲ A monk praying for peace; one tradition states that Chandragupta became a monk.

Event: Limiting Greek expansion.

Role: Indian general Chandragupta organized resistance to Greek rule following Alexander the Great's conquest of the Punjab (in present-day Pakistan and western India). Chandragupta later won control of the rest of India, becoming the first emperor to unite the land under a single ruler.

Taxila. Taxila lay hundreds of miles to the west, on the other side of India in the area called the Punjab. At that time, it was India's leading educational center, where kings and nobles sent their sons to learn all subjects, including the arts of war. Chanakya felt that an important destiny awaited Chandragupta, and he arranged for the prince to receive the best possible education.

Participation: Limiting Greek Expansion

Sign of Greatness

One legend has it that young Chandragupta actually met Alexander in person. The two spoke, and something that the bold prince said angered Alexander, who then ordered him killed. But Chandragupta escaped, outrunning his captors. He ran for some time through the countryside, until finally, exhausted, he fell asleep. As he slept, a huge lion approached him, licked the sweat from his body, and then gently woke him up before walking off. Since lions were symbols of royalty, Chandragupta interpreted the experience as another sign that he would one day be a king. He was then inspired to build an army that would overthrow Greek rule.

Alexander the Great. Sometime during his military training, Chandragupta had the chance to observe **Alexander the Great** (see entry), one of the finest generals of them all, in action. It was about 326 B.C., and Chandragupta was a young man of around nineteen or twenty. Alexander's army had marched all the way from Greece and conquered much of the Punjab. If his exhausted and homesick troops had not forced him to turn back, Alexander could easily have taken over all of India.

Dhana Nanda. Magadha—Chandragupta's birthplace and the most powerful kingdom in India—was ruled in the early decades of the fourth century B.C. by a very unpopular king named Dhana Nanda. His enemies held that he was the son of a barber and had no legitimate claim to the throne. Dhana Nanda was well known for hoarding the treasure of his eastern Indian territory and ignoring the needs of his people. Chanakya, who had been employed by Dhana Nanda but was unjustly fired prior to visiting Chandragupta's village, sought revenge against the corrupt king—and felt that his promising young student could help him gain it.

Alexander's successors. Chandragupta began his career as a military leader in the Punjab, the area of western India where Alexander conducted his seemingly unstoppable march of conquest. The kings of the Punjab had surrendered one by one to Alexander, until about 325 B.C., when the entire region was his. He left several of his generals behind to take charge of the administration of Greek rule there. Then, two years later, Alexander died, leaving no heirs. Throughout his empire, his generals became his successors, taking power for themselves if they could and fighting over the pieces of a crumbling empire.

Forming an army. In the Punjab, however, even before Alexander's death, Chandragupta had begun assembling the Indians for a rebellion against the Greeks. He realized that the Indians' greatest weakness was their lack of unity. The various kings of the small kingdoms in the Punjab had failed to join forces, and many of the region's towns and cities were not even part of any specific kingdom. These *arashtrakas,* or "kingless" communities, were more numerous than the established kingdoms of India and provided Chandragupta with an eager army to take on the Greeks.

Overthrowing Greek rule. As he built up his forces, Chandragupta also began planning other methods of resistance against the Greeks. Alexander had divided his Indian territory into six provinces, each governed by a general. In 326 B.C., just after Alexander's departure from the area, Indian fighters assassinated one of the generals. The next year another suffered the same fate. Others followed. The assassinations were carried out in secret, but some modern historians see Chandragupta as the mastermind behind them. Two years later, when Alexander himself died, open revolution broke out.

Alexander's fragile empire. Throughout the mid-320s B.C., Greek generals struggled to maintain control of the empire's farthest reaches in India, but the assassinations continued and Indian kings assumed power. After pulling out of India, Alexander was too far away to maintain a firm grip on the area. His death was the final blow to the already troubled Greek domination of India. Alexander's empire was defeated not only by its own huge size but also by Chandragupta's leadership. Chandragupta had successfully organized the Punjab kingdoms and the Indian military.

Attack on Magadha. By 321 B.C., Chandragupta had totally freed the Punjab from the Greeks. Now, with a strong army under his command, he turned his attention eastward to Magadha, overthrowing Dhana Nanda and occupying the capital city of Pataliputra. He then executed Dhana Nanda, took Magadha's throne himself, and appointed his old friend Chanakya as his prime minister. Chanakya had thus lived to achieve his revenge on Dhana Nanda.

A growing empire for Chandragupta. Over the next fifteen years, Chandragupta expanded his power over much of the rest of India. He returned to the Punjab, claiming his right to rule both the *arashtrakas* and the kingdoms there. He also pushed south into central India, conquering many of that region's kingdoms. It was the first time that most of India had been claimed by one ruler, an emperor who could demand the obedience of kings.

Seleucus. Just west of Chandragupta's Indian empire lay Bactria (present-day Afghanistan), which had also been conquered by Alexander. Around 304 B.C. it was under the rule of Seleucus, a Macedonian general who had won the eastern part of Alexander's empire. Soon after reclaiming Bactria, Seleucus attempted to win the Indian territory that Alexander had conquered two decades earlier. From Bactria he ventured into the Punjab.

But Seleucus met a strong and unified empire under a single, effective ruler. Faced by Chandragupta's powerful army, he soon turned from invader to negotiator: in the end, Seleucus agreed to give up territory west of the Punjab.

Ancient Legends

Most details of Chandragupta's life have passed into the realm of legend, as the stories about his childhood show. Like Alexander, he was a conqueror who inspired romantic tales, sometimes with a strong element of the supernatural. Many of these tales are part of India's religious traditions, for Chandragupta and his successors were important religious figures as well as emperors. Greek authors such as Plutarch, who wrote about Alexander, also mention Chandragupta, calling him Sandrocottus.

Aftermath

Retirement. Around 300 B.C., while still only in his forties, Chandragupta retired, leaving his empire to his son, Bindusara. The king then became a follower of Jainism—a religion of nonviolence toward all living things. One tradition states that he became a monk, living in a cave to pursue a life of religious meditation.

Another states that he fasted to death, in sorrow for a raging famine, in 297 B.C.

Mauryan dynasty. Chandragupta had taken the family name Maurya, and the Mauryan dynasty (ruling family) that he founded went on to become one of the most influential in Indian history. Both Bindusara and his son, Asoka, added territory to the empire, so that it occupied the entire Indian subcontinent by the time of Asoka's death in 232 B.C.

Model government. The Mauryan empire broke up soon after Asoka died. Greeks from Bactria again invaded from the west, Asian nomads swept in from the east, and central kingdoms reclaimed their independence. But even in the turmoil of succeeding centuries, the Mauryan rulers provided a model of strong central authority for future kings and emperors to follow.

For More Information

Gopal, Lallanji. *Chandragupta Maurya.* New Delhi, India: National Book Trust, 1968.

Mookerji, Radha Kumud. *Chandragupta Maurya and His Times.* Delhi, India: Rajkamal Publications, 1952.

Gifts to the Defeated

Having won the respect of his powerful neighbor, Chandragupta made an effort to keep up good relations, sending Seleucus a gift of five hundred war elephants. Elephants have been called the tanks of the ancient world, and the gift helped Seleucus win an important battle against another of Alexander's generals. After that, peace prevailed between the two empires.

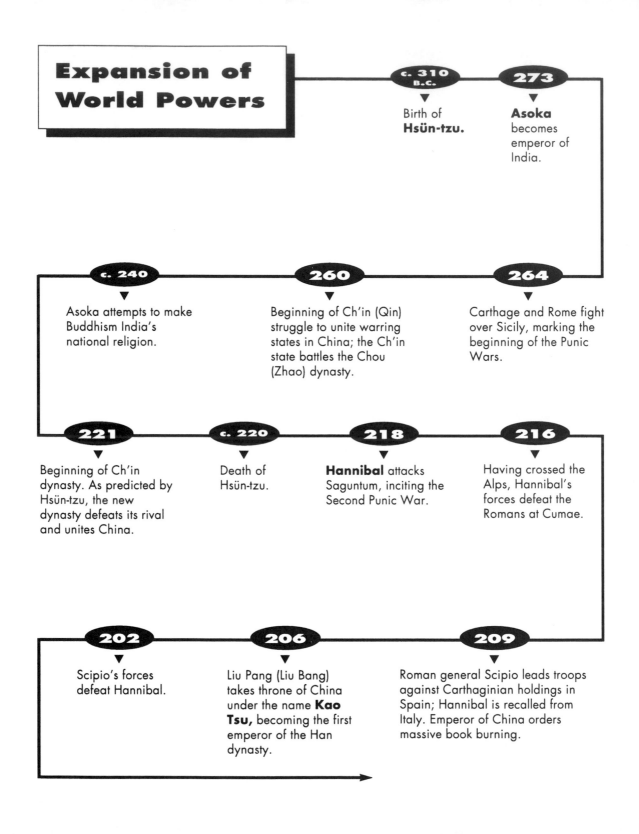

Expansion of World Powers

c. 310 B.C.
Birth of **Hsün-tzu.**

273
Asoka becomes emperor of India.

c. 240
Asoka attempts to make Buddhism India's national religion.

260
Beginning of Ch'in (Qin) struggle to unite warring states in China; the Ch'in state battles the Chou (Zhao) dynasty.

264
Carthage and Rome fight over Sicily, marking the beginning of the Punic Wars.

221
Beginning of Ch'in dynasty. As predicted by Hsün-tzu, the new dynasty defeats its rival and unites China.

c. 220
Death of Hsün-tzu.

218
Hannibal attacks Saguntum, inciting the Second Punic War.

216
Having crossed the Alps, Hannibal's forces defeat the Romans at Cumae.

202
Scipio's forces defeat Hannibal.

206
Liu Pang (Liu Bang) takes throne of China under the name **Kao Tsu,** becoming the first emperor of the Han dynasty.

209
Roman general Scipio leads troops against Carthaginian holdings in Spain; Hannibal is recalled from Italy. Emperor of China orders massive book burning.

EXPANSION OF WORLD POWERS

The period from about 270 to 200 B.C. was marked by the acquisition of new land and the reorganization of governments in several parts of the world. Rome, India, and China all took control of their smaller neighbors and developed large empires.

Rome. A chief competitor of Rome for control of the Mediterranean trade routes was Carthage, a trade center in northern Africa. As early as 264 B.C., Carthage and Rome were engaged in the First Punic War, a squabble that began over control of a city then known as Messana (now Messina) on the island of Sicily. In the sporadic scuffling that lasted more than two dozen years, Rome took charge of the islands of Corsica and Sardinia and destroyed Carthage's power in Sicily. These three islands became the first provinces of Roman expansion. This first war left a legacy of bitterness between the two old powers. **Hannibal** was among the Carthaginians who swore revenge against the Romans.

Taking over the rule of a section of Spain from his father, Hannibal deliberately seized a Roman city, Saguntum, inciting the Second Punic War in 218 B.C. He then crossed over the Alps into Roman territory and was enjoying considerable success until forced to return to Spain by the threats of the army of Roman

Hannibal directing his army with its caravan of elephants across the Alps; fifty-nine thousand soldiers and thirty-seven elephants began the trek, uncertain of what lay ahead.

general Publius Scipio. Again the Roman forces were victorious and drove Carthage to surrender all its colonies.

Finally, in a third war (149-146 B.C.), Carthage was totally defeated and the city itself destroyed. That left the Roman Empire free to contend with another rebel state, Macedonia. After defeating the Syria-supported king of Macedonia, the Romans continued into Asia Minor. By 44 B.C. the Roman Empire had expanded to include Greece and the lands of ancient Ionia. It had also gained control of present-day France, nearly all of Spain, and much of the coast of Africa. Although the empire continued to grow for several more decades, the death of Julius Caesar in 44 B.C. marked the end of rapid Roman expansion.

India. About two decades before the beginning of the Punic Wars, Chandragupta, the first great organizer of India, died. His grandson and eventual successor, **Asoka,** continued his plan to expand the Mauryan empire and went on to initiate political and religious reforms to unify the Indian people. Around 240 B.C., as the traditional Hindu religion was losing its fire, Asoka accepted Buddhism and tried to make it a state religion. In the end, he succeeded neither in establishing a lasting empire nor in replacing Hinduism. Buddhism did, however, force Hinduism into reform, and the latter religion regained its dominant position in India, while Buddhism gained greater strength in other Asian nations. Shortly after Asoka's death, the great Indian empire started by his grandfather and completed in his lifetime disintegrated into a new array of small kingdoms.

China. In the third century B.C., a philosopher named **Hsün-tzu** (also spelled Xunzi) appeared in China, which at that time was only a loose confederacy of several independent states. While studying the old works of Confucius, Hsün-tzu became an adviser to royal houses in the Chinese states. He warned against the growing power of the state of Ch'in (also spelled Qin), which eventually gained control of the other Chinese states. But the Ch'in dynasty, or period of rule, did not last long. In 206 B.C. Liu Pang (or Liu Bang), a minor government official, succeeded in overthrowing the Ch'in emperor and revived China. Liu Pang took the name **Kao Tsu** (or Gaozu) and became the first ruler of the Han dynasty. This dynasty, which lasted for more than four centuries, was so powerful and organized so much Chinese territory under one rule that most Chinese today claim to have Han ancestry.

Asoka

c. 306-c. 232 B.C.

Personal Background

Royal beginning. The grandson of the first Mauryan emperor, Chandragupta, Asoka (also spelled Ashoka) was born around 306 B.C. in ancient India and raised according to the teachings of the Hindu religion. His mother, Subhadrangi, was the daughter of a Brahman, or Hindu priest, and his father, Bindusara, was the ruling emperor. Legend has it that the royal family was enormous and that Asoka had as many as ninety-nine brothers and sisters.

Education. Asoka was apparently highly educated and learned most of the dialects spoken in India, including Prakrit, as well as Greek and Aramaic, a Middle Eastern language. As a young man, he was appointed to various government positions by his father. In the 280s to 270s B.C., Asoka became viceroy, or governor, of Taxila, a large city and center of commerce and education in India. His experience in the politically important region helped prepare him to assume the emperor's seat in 273.

Viceroy. During his tenure as viceroy of Taxila, Asoka learned government procedure and received his first lessons in diplomacy. He had been sent to the area to quiet a revolt led by its citizens, who apparently felt oppressed by the higher officials of the Mauryan empire. Asoka successfully ended the uprising and in doing so helped solidify Mauryan power in India. As a reward

▲ **Fragment of an inscription on Buddhism Asoka ordered to be engraved on a stone pillar at Sarnath.**

Event: Uniting India.

Role: As the third emperor of the Mauryas, Asoka united India through his dedication to the Buddhist philosophy of the dharma, or law of piety. Both an able statesman and spiritual guide, he earned distinction for his promotion of such concepts as nonviolence, generosity, religious tolerance, and respect for all forms of life.

for his efforts, Asoka was appointed viceroy of Ujjain, where he married Devi, the daughter of a local merchant. They had at least two children. Devi is thought to have been a Buddhist who helped spur Asoka's conversion to that religion, but evidence of this assertion remains inconclusive.

Taking the throne. In 273 B.C. Asoka's father died and he inherited the throne. He was not officially crowned, however, until 269 B.C. It appears that tremendous infighting was being waged between Asoka and his brothers as to who would become emperor. This quarreling caused the four-year delay in officially naming Bindusara's successor. Although some scholars believe that Asoka killed six of his older brothers in order to gain the throne, these reports are largely unsubstantiated.

Another Side to Asoka?

Some historians insist that as a young man Asoka was a brutal leader known as "Asoka the Wicked" (Smith, p. 23). While this theory is purely speculative, it may have been spread to further sensationalize and contrast with the emperor's eventual renunciation of violence.

Kalinga. Eight years after he was officially made the third Mauryan emperor, Asoka began a war to take Kalinga, a strategically important township located on the coast of the Bay of Bengal. At the time, he had intentions of expanding his empire and increasing his power through force and warfare.

The Kalinga War proved to be the single most important event in Asoka's life and signaled a major turning point in his development. An especially bloody conflict, it resulted in the deaths of 100,000 people; another 150,000 were taken prisoner. When Asoka visited the battlefield and witnessed the brutal slaughter firsthand, he was greatly distressed and is said to have written:

> Thus arose His Majesty's remorse for having conquered the Kalingas, because the conquest of a country previously unconquered involves the slaughter, death, and carrying away of captive people. That is a matter of profound sorrow and regret to His Sacred Majesty. (Asoka in Smith, p. 25)

Participation: Uniting India

Buddhist monk. As if divinely inspired, Asoka completely abandoned his policy of war and began his conversion to Buddhism, a religion promoting nonviolence. He joined the Buddhist order of monks known as the Sangha and established a monastic temple. Over the next four years, while serving as the temple's leader, he studied Buddhist philosophy. By 257 B.C. Asoka was issuing edicts, or moral sermons, to educate the population in proper conduct. He carved these orders in stone on pillars and rocks throughout India and wrote them in various regional dialects in order to reach all segments of the population.

Dharma. Asoka's edicts—which were not laws, but rather suggestions as to how to live one's life in peace and harmony—promoted the concept of "dharma" (later known as "dhamma"). Dharma has been described as the law of piety (being dutiful or devout), but in simple terms means a policy of social responsibility. Asoka is said to have believed that the practice of dharma involved "little sin, many good deeds, mercifulness, charity, truthfulness, and purity" (Sen, p. 146). His edicts encouraged people to become vegetarians, respect all forms of human life, tolerate other religions, and generally treat humanity and the earth with respect. In his Pillar Edict 4, for instance, he states that people should "bear in mind what causes happiness or pain and be devoted to the Dharma" (Sen, p. 150). Asoka also urged people to "act rightly" and eliminate feelings of envy, anger, cruelty, indifference, and laziness—feelings that might lead to evil deeds, pain, or even war (Sen, p. 110).

> ### H. G. Wells's Six Greatest Men of History
>
> British author H. G. Wells called Emperor Asoka "one of the Six Greatest Men of History" because "he is the only military monarch on record who abandoned warfare after victory." The other five great men on Wells's list include Siddhartha Gautama, or the Buddha, the founder of Buddhism; Greek philosophers Socrates and Aristotle; English Franciscan philosopher Roger Bacon; and U.S. president Abraham Lincoln. (Sen, p. iii)

Buddhism expands. Centuries before Jesus Christ or Muhammad began to teach, Asoka's edicts were considered truly revolutionary and had a deep influence on India and the world. Serving as both a spiritual guide and head of state, Asoka converted the majority of India's fifty million inhabitants from Hinduism to Buddhism. He sent missionaries throughout the world to establish Buddhism as a major world religion, and Buddhist influence soon spread to other nations, including Tibet, China, and southeast Asia.

▲ Laotian political leaders offering food and flowers to Buddhist monks as they parade during opening ceremonies of Buddhist Lent in July 1963.

Once converted to Buddhism, Asoka became a humble leader. He did not seek glory for himself but hoped only to promote the concept of dharma. In his Rock Edict 10 he states: "[I do] not consider glory or fame to be productive of any great value ... except that ... at the present time and in the future, my subjects may practise respectfulness towards the Dharma and may follow the practise of the Dharma. For this alone ... [I desire] glory or fame" (Sen, p. 90).

Unity. Under Asoka's leadership, the Indian empire was unified into a single political unit and the country prospered economically and socially. The emperor based the economy on trade and agriculture and established strong ties with the Roman Empire in Europe. Art, education, prosperity, and peace flourished during his tenure. Among his most important political moves were his support for the education of women, an increase in road and building construction throughout the country, the planting of huge fields of medicinal herbs, the banning of animal sacrifices, and his outlawing the killing of animals for food.

Public opinion. In an effort to stay close to the people he governed and understand their problems, Asoka traveled often and extensively throughout the Indian empire. A pioneer on the political front, he sent out emissaries to gauge public opinion concerning his policies. This early "polling" process allowed him to understand citizens' regional and individual concerns.

Aftermath

Long reign. Emperor Asoka ruled India for thirty-seven years and during that time issued at least thirty-five edicts. Written in stone, the edicts were found in gathering places throughout virtually every region of the empire. During his long and influential reign, Asoka succeeded in unifying a vast and multicultural India. Like **Kao Tsu** (see entry), the first emperor of the Han dynasty (ruling family) in China, Asoka considered all Indians his "children" and took on the role of father figure, offering moral advice as well as implementing law.

Asoka died in 232 B.C. and was succeeded by his son, Kunala. The Indian empire began to decline in the ensuing years, and war broke out once more. Until his edicts were translated into English in 1837 by English anthropologist James Prinsep, Asoka was virtually forgotten and unknown in the West. Today he is widely revered throughout the world as one of the most influential leaders in history.

For More Information

Sen, Amulyachandra. *Asoka's Edicts*. Calcutta: Bani Munshi, 1956.

Smith, Vincent A. *Asoka: The Buddhist Emperor of China*. New York: Clarendon Press, 1909.

Thapar, Romila. *Asoka and the Decline of the Mauryas*. Oxford, England: Oxford University Press, 1961.

Hsün-tzu

c. 310-220 B.C.

Personal Background

Hsün-tzu (pronounced "**soon** zee"; also spelled Xunzi) was born in the northern state of Chou (also spelled Zhao) sometime around 310 B.C. He was named Hsün K'uang, Hsü being his family name, K'uang his given name. Later he was known as Hsü Ch'ing, or Minister Hsün, because he once held the government office of provincial minister. Only later in life, or perhaps not until after his death, was he called Hsün-tzu, which means "Master Hsün."

Warring states. Hsün-tzu grew up during China's Warring States period. Around 500 B.C., nearly two centuries before his birth, China consisted of about 150 small independent states, each ruled by a single powerful family. One hundred years later, when the Warring States period began, only seven or eight large consolidated states remained. One of them was Chou. For the next two centuries, these large states battled each other. Hsün-tzu witnessed the growth in power of Ch'in (also spelled Qin), Chou's formidable neighbor to the west. By the time he died around 220 B.C., the state of Ch'in had finally won out, conquering the last of its neighbors. China was united under one ruler.

Jixia Academy. The unification of the warring states was far from complete in 295 B.C., when fifteen-year-old Hsün-tzu traveled east to the state of Chi (Qi) to enter the Jixia Academy, ancient China's leading center of learning. He was young to be leaving

▲ **A Chinese warrior praying before Buddha; Hsün-tzu learned about the many different philosophies on the rise during and just before the Warring States era.**

Event: Shaping the ideas of Confucius.

Role: Just as Aristotle built on the works of earlier Greek philosophers to create a body of knowledge that shaped Western thought for centuries, Hsün-tzu helped shape the ideas of Confucius into a system that would come to dominate generations of Chinese thought and behavior.

home at all, and especially young to be studying at such a well-known institution, but his scholastic achievement was remarkable enough to warrant his acceptance there. At Jixia (pronounced "**jees** yah"), Hsün-tzu learned about the many different philosophies on the rise during and just before the Warring States era, which later came to be called the period of the "hundred schools" of thought. He also studied rhetoric, or the art of effective communication. At the time, rhetoric in China was geared toward influencing a ruler's decisions; the arguments used were called *shuo,* or "persuasions."

Participation: Shaping the Ideas of Confucius

Tian Wen. Hsün-tzu's studies at the Jixia Academy probably lasted eight to ten years, until 286 B.C. When he left the academy in his mid-twenties, he tried to apply what he had learned to the real world by offering his advice to a government official in the state of Chi. His writings about the encounter indicate that he met with some opposition.

Hsün-tzu wrote his ill-fated persuasion to an aristocratic prime minister of Chi named Tian Wen. Apparently Hsün-tzu saw that Tian Wen—a cousin of the state's King Min—was using Min's unpopularity to strengthen his own position and threaten the royal grip on power. The young philosopher advised Tian Wen against this type of strategy, backing his argument with past examples of power struggles that had weakened a state and left it open to invasion from stronger neighbors. But Tian Wen refused to listen. Soon after, as Hsün-tzu had foretold, an alliance of neighboring states did invade Chi, crushing King Min's armies. Min was later tortured to death, and Tian Wen was forced to flee. The Jixia Academy was also ruined, as its teachers fled from the invading forces.

Early works. Hsün-tzu wrote several works during the period of destabilization in Chi. One called "On Strengthening the State" was drawn from the unsuccessful persuasion he had prepared for Tian Wen. Three other pieces he wrote while in Chi deal with issues in philosophy. One, *Jiebi,* or "Dispelling Blindness," argues against the ideas of some earlier philosophers from the "hundred schools." Another, *Zhenglun,* or "Rectifying Theses," similarly criticizes other philosophers of Hsün-tzu's own time. The third, *Zhongni,* or "On Confucius," marks Hsün-tzu's first attempt to write about the ideas of Confucius, the esteemed Chinese philosopher who lived from 551 to 479 B.C. *Zhongni* reveals Hsün-tzu's support of the Confucian tradition.

Chu and Ch'in. In about 283 B.C. Hsün-tzu settled briefly in the southern state of Chu and began composing a body of writings that would establish him as a leading philosopher. These works dealt with conflicts he witnessed between Chu and its aggressive neighbor to the west, Ch'in. Hsün-tzu determined that Ch'in might one day conquer all of China. "When Qin orders Chu to move to the left," he observed, "it feels obliged to move left, and when Qin orders it to move right, it is obliged to move right" (Hsün-tzu in Knoblock, p. 8).

Hsün-tzu began to question the use of raw power by a state such as Ch'in; power, he explained, could be abused. "When the techniques of power have reached their goal, one must put into practice the arts of justice." To be truly effective, he argued, a government must be run by "gentlemen who are upright, sincere, trustworthy, and complete" (Hsün-tzu in Knoblock, pp. 8-9).

The "Confucian gentleman." The idea of a "gentleman," or *junzi* (also translated as "superior man" or "noble man"), is especially important to the philosophy of Confucianism. The *junzi* was a man whose behavior was guided by *li* (often translated as "ritual" or "proper conduct"). Based on ancient Chinese writings, *li* called for certain standards of behavior to be observed on the basis of one's role in society. "Let the ruler rule as he should," Confucius said, "and the minister be a minister as he should. Let the father be a father as he should and the son act as a son should" (Confucius in Fairbank, p. 52). In addition, according to Confucius, only proper behavior could endow political leaders with the authority to rule: "When a prince's personal conduct is correct, his government is effective without the issuing of orders. If his personal conduct is not correct, he may issue orders but they will not be obeyed" (Fairbank, pp. 52-53).

Return to Jixia. Hsün-tzu returned to Jixia sometime around 275 B.C., when he was in his mid-thirties. In Chu, he had continued his writings about Confucius and about how to apply Confucian ideas to the conflicts that were tearing at his nation. Back at Jixia, he began to add his own ideas to the Confucian tradition.

Confucius's best-known follower at the time was a Chinese sage named Meng-tzu (also called Mencius). Meng-tzu had argued that human nature was basically good, and that evil or selfish acts stemmed from bad influences on the personality from the outside world. Hsün-tzu disagreed. He believed that goodness did not necessarily come naturally to all human beings; people needed teachers, or models, to help them see how they should behave. He expressed this idea most forcibly in the *Jing'e,* the title of which is translated as "Man's Nature Is Evil."

Journey to Ch'in. Hsün-tzu was the Jixia Academy's leading scholar during the mid-270s and 260s B.C. But he had sparked dissension and made enemies with his controversial teachings. The spread of false accusations against him prompted him to leave Jixia, probably sometime around 265 B.C.

Hsün-tzu next traveled to Ch'in, the large western state with seemingly unmatchable power over its neighbors. He met with Ch'in's king and prime minister, putting forth his views about the role Confucian ideas should play in politics. But the strength and efficiency of the state of Ch'in totally contradicted Confucian thought on the rise of effective government. Unlike states such as Chi and Chu, Ch'in lacked a strong tradition of education and scholarship. Hsün-tzu argued that Confucian scholars were necessary to the state—that without them, leaders would have no way of ruling in accordance with *li.* The rulers of Ch'in had no regard for *li,* yet they had achieved extraordinary success. Because of this, Hsün-tzu's faith in the soundness of Confucian ideas was understandably shaken.

Defeat of Ch'in. Around 260 B.C. the Ch'in army attacked Hsün-tzu's native state of Chou, where he had returned to live a year or two earlier. The king of the nearby state of Wei promised to send help to Chou forces but—fearing reprisal from the Ch'in government—halted his soldiers at the border. However, Wei Wuji, the Wei king's younger brother, took unauthorized command of the army and crossed the border, arriving just as Chou's army was going into battle. Almost simultaneously, an army from Chu under the leadership of Huang Xie arrived for further reinforcement. Together, they totally defeated the invading Ch'in army.

Wei Wuji's decision to cross the border against his brother's wishes led to the defeat of Ch'in. Hsün-tzu's belief in the power of Confucianism was renewed: Wei Wuji was the perfect example of a *junzi,* or Confucian "superior man." He had made the right decision in the face of a challenge. Though he disobeyed the words of his brother, he actually served the state well by insisting on doing what he knew was right.

Minister and teacher. Sometime in the 250s B.C., Hsün-tzu accepted a position as minister of the province of Lanling in the state of Chu. He held the office on and off for about twenty years while continuing to lecture and write philosophy books. He had become China's most famous teacher, and his students went on to successes of their own. Especially notable was Li Si, who became an adviser to the rulers of Ch'in in the 240s B.C., when Ch'in power was again on the rise.

Aftermath

Retirement. In 238 B.C. Ch'in rulers assassinated Huang Xie, the Chu leader who had commanded forces at Chou and had later given Hsün-tzu his post as minister. Wei Wuji, the other strong opponent of Ch'in power, had died a half dozen years earlier. After Huang's death, there were no able leaders left to guide the opposition to Ch'in. Hsün-tzu—by this time dismissed from his post—watched as one by one Ch'in conquered all the remaining states in China. The last fell in 221 B.C., shortly before Hsün-tzu died at the age of ninety.

For More Information

Fairbank, John King. *China: A New History.* Cambridge, Massachusetts: Harvard University Press, 1992.

Knoblock, John. *Hsün-tzu: A Translation and Study of the Complete Works.* Volume 1. Stanford, California: Stanford University Press, 1988.

Hannibal

247-183 B.C.

Personal Background

Early life. Hannibal Barca, the eldest of four sons in the family of General Hamilcar Barca, was born in 247 B.C. in the ancient trading city of Carthage, located on northern Africa's Mediterranean coast (near present-day Tunis, Tunisia). Carthage was a wealthy city-state that controlled a vast empire along the Mediterranean Sea. Through treaty and trade, it exerted its influence over most of western North Africa, southern Spain, Sardinia, Corsica, and western Sicily.

Rome: An inherited enemy. Rome, the most powerful Mediterranean city-state, became Carthage's main competitor for control of the Mediterranean. Rome had recently conquered the whole Italian peninsula, and from 500 through 146 B.C. the two rivals warred continually, particularly over the island of Sicily, which was situated directly between them.

Carthage. Born during the first of the Punic Wars, a series of wars between Rome and Carthage, Hannibal was taught from an early age that the Roman Republic was an enemy. His father instilled in him a deep distrust of the Romans. Legend has it that Hamilcar actually made his son swear an oath against Rome just before taking him on a military expedition to Spain. Placing his hand on a sacrificial animal, nine-year-old Hannibal swore that the

▲ Hannibal

Event: Challenging the Roman Republic.

Role: One of the most celebrated military leaders in history, Carthaginian commander Hannibal overcame great odds and battled successfully for fifteen years against the much larger and more powerful Roman army. He succeeded in capturing most of the southwest Italian coast and nearly defeated the Roman army on its home soil several times between 218 and 216 B.C. before finally losing to Rome fourteen years later.

Roman Republic would always be his "deadly enemy" (de Beer, p. 95). This was an oath he did not take lightly.

Destined to lead. In addition to becoming a sworn enemy of Rome, Hannibal was expected to follow in his father's footsteps and become a military leader. Along with his brothers Hasdrubal, Hanno, and Mago, Hannibal was taught to ride horses, clean and carry weapons and armor, and fight with knives and swords—all in preparation for an eventual clash with the mighty Roman army. Though the First Punic War ended in 241 B.C. when Hannibal was six, Hamilcar was certain that Rome and Carthage would again take up arms against each other. He intended to lead the second attack himself.

Education. According to Roman poet and historian Livy, Hannibal had a keen interest in the military and showed talent as a soldier. He excelled at horsemanship, had a mind for strategy and tactics, and was a natural leader. Hannibal also developed an interest in Greek mythology and philosophy and learned to both speak and write the language.

Spain: The plan. While still a child, Hannibal moved with his father to Spain to help build Carthaginian power there. Hamilcar then planned to launch an attack on Rome. Only a few years earlier, Carthage had lost the First Punic War to Rome and, as a result, lost control of Sicily and Sardinia. This established Rome as the dominant sea power in the Mediterranean and made Italy very hard to attack from the coast.

Determined to find a way to defeat the Romans and crush their empire, Hamilcar drew up a plan for a land assault. He would lead his army northeast through Spain and present-day France, cross the rugged, mountainous regions of the Pyrenees and the Alps, and surprise the Romans by attacking them in northern Italy.

Hamilcar died before he could put his scheme into action. In 228 B.C. Hasdrubal the Handsome, Hannibal's brother-in-law,

---

Foretelling Hannibal's Feats

In Virgil's epic *The Aeneid,* the goddess Dido kills herself because her true love, Aeneas, deserts her in Carthage when he sets out to found Rome. Just before she dies, Dido vows revenge against all Romans and foretells of an "Avenger" from Carthage who will one day challenge the Roman Republic. This "Avenger" was Hannibal. (de Beer, p. 54)

▲ Hannibal with his elephants crossing the Rhone River, in the Alps; the three-week journey to Italy proved fatal for more than half of Hannibal's army.

became the Carthaginian general in Spain. He picked up where Hamilcar left off but in the midst of his efforts was murdered. In 221 B.C., when he was only in his mid-twenties, Hannibal inherited the Carthaginian command and began laying the groundwork to carry out his father's plan.

Participation:
Challenging the Roman Republic

Building an army. Unlike the Romans, who were drafted into military service and could easily be replaced, the Carthaginians hired professional soldiers, or mercenaries, to do their fighting for them. One of Hannibal's first tasks as general was to increase his army to sixty thousand men and train them for the surprise attack. He recruited soldiers from Carthage, Spain, Gaul (present-day France), Algeria, Morocco, the Balearic Islands, and Numidia (present-day Algeria). In a telling display of his management skills, Hannibal organized his mercenary army into a fierce fighting force. He built friendship and confidence among the diverse group, thereby consolidating Carthaginian power in Spain. From 221 to 219 B.C., his troops captured a series of wealthy Spanish towns, and the spoils—including gold, silver, and weapons—were divided among the soldiers.

The Elephant in War

Large Indian and smaller forest elephants of North Africa were used by the Carthaginian military like modern-day tanks. They bulldozed through trees, paving the way for troops. They also carried soldiers—usually archers—on their backs, and charged against opposing forces. The elephants were a frightening sight, especially to those who had never seen the likes of them before.

Despite his status as a general, Hannibal wore the simple uniform of a rank-and-file soldier. He fought alongside his men and slept on the ground, refusing the comforts a general usually received. Inspired by his example and confident in his leadership, by 219 B.C. the Carthaginian army was ready to embark on the difficult journey over the Alps to take on the much larger Roman army.

Hannibal needed approval from the Carthaginian senate before venturing into Italy. Because the Carthaginians had lost the First Punic War, most senators were not in favor of challenging Rome again. Anticipating government resistance, Hannibal opted to avoid a senatorial confrontation by luring the Romans into declaring war first.

Attack on Saguntum. Hannibal set his plan in motion by attacking the town of Saguntum in Spain, which was allied with Rome. As he suspected, the citizens of Saguntum appealed to Rome for help, and the Romans promptly demanded that Hannibal surrender. Hannibal, meanwhile, informed his government that the conflict was strictly a matter between Carthage and Saguntum and that he had no quarrel with Rome; Rome's involvement, he insisted, would constitute a declaration of war on Carthage. In the spring of 218 B.C., the Second Punic or "Hannibalic" War officially began when Rome came to the aid of Saguntum.

Marriage. Around the same time, Hannibal married a Spanish princess named Imilce, who may have been of Greek descent.

During the siege of Saguntum, their son was born. Little is known about either of them. It appears that Hannibal spent less than a year with his wife and child before sending them back to Carthage when the Second Punic War began. It is believed that he did not see them again for seventeen years—if ever.

The plan in action. In May 218 B.C., equipped with swords, spears, heavy shields, and armor, Hannibal's army began its march into history. Fifty-nine thousand soldiers (fifty thousand infantry; nine thousand cavalry) and thirty-seven elephants began the fifteen-hundred-kilometer trek toward Piedmont, Italy, uncertain of what lay ahead.

Heavy losses. The three-week journey to Italy proved fatal for more than half of Hannibal's army. Not only did he lose men to hostile tribes they encountered along the way, but a huge number of soldiers and animals died from the effects of the harsh weather and accidents along the rugged terrain. Though it was nearly summer, snow and ice still covered the Alps, which made crossing very difficult. In addition, there were no roads, only narrow trails through the mountain passes. Many men, horses, and elephants tumbled to their deaths from the steep cliffs and slippery rocks. By the time they reached Piedmont, the Carthaginian army numbered just twenty-nine thousand. Though in dire need of reinforcements and supplies, they still remained a formidable opponent.

Shortly after arriving in northern Italy, Hannibal's troops engaged in their first battle with the Roman army. The general's strategy was simple: strike unexpectedly and move on quickly, which he did with great success.

Scipio. Led by Consul Publius Cornelius Scipio, the Romans were indeed surprised when the Carthaginians arrived in northern Italy. But Scipio was convinced Hannibal's small army could "be nothing but a rabble ... frost-bitten and lame" after crossing the Alps (de Beer, p. 185). He soon changed his mind. Six thousand Carthaginians attacked two thousand Romans outside of Piedmont and slaughtered them. Scipio was hurt badly and had to be rescued by his son.

Taking the Po Valley. With Scipio severely wounded, the Roman command passed to its co-consul, Tiberius Sempronius

Longus, who repeated Scipio's mistake: he, too, underestimated Hannibal. Rather than proceeding cautiously, Sempronius attacked Hannibal at the Trebbia River in northern Italy. In a confusing battle that took place during a violent rainstorm, Hannibal forced Sempronius to retreat.

Nearly sixty thousand Gauls seeking independence from the Roman Republic then joined Hannibal, providing much-needed reinforcements. With his fortified army, Hannibal proceeded to conquer towns throughout northern Italy's Po Valley, working his way south. Striking like a "thunderbolt," he raided Roman trading posts and rapidly increased his weapon and gold supply (de Beer, p. 188).

Lake Trasimene. In the spring of 217 B.C., Hannibal launched a successful attack at Lake Trasimene in central Italy by first advancing into the Arno Valley. Illustrating his talent for strategy, he lured nearly fifteen thousand Romans into the basin of Saguineto, where his soldiers were waiting in the hills. When the Romans rode into the trap, the Carthaginians sprang from their hiding places, completely surrounding the Romans. In three hours they killed them all, including the newly elected Roman consul, Caius Nepos Flaminius. Though Hannibal lost eighteen hundred men and the sight in one eye during the battle, Lake Trasimene was a huge victory for the Carthaginians. They were well on their way to winning the war.

Cumae. Hannibal needed to capture a seaport in order to communicate with Carthage and obtain additional reinforcements to crush the Roman Republic. He set his sights on the fertile coastal towns of Neapolis (Naples) and nearby Cumae, where he found supplies as well as ships. The Romans assumed Hannibal would attack Rome, but he surprised them by attacking Italy's southwest coast.

Regarded by many historians as the first substantial victory for Hannibal, the battle of Cumae, which took place in 216 B.C., nearly signaled the end for the Roman Republic. While Hannibal

◄ **Hannibal is one of the most celebrated military strategists in history.**

lost six thousand soldiers, Rome lost seventy thousand, including another Roman consul. As a symbol of his undeniable conquest, Hannibal sent three bushels of gold rings—all taken from the fingers of slain Roman soldiers—back to Carthage. The Romans were defeated so badly that nearby towns are said to have defected to his side.

Hannibal hoped his success at Cumae would inspire the Carthaginian senate to send him the reinforcements he had requested. However, the government of Carthage greatly undervalued Hannibal's military advancements; many scholars feel the city-state probably missed a golden opportunity to topple Rome when it was at its weakest.

The end. For the next fifteen years, the Second Punic War raged on. Because he never received reinforcements, Hannibal was unable to hold anything more than the southwest coast of Italy. In 209 B.C. the Romans began recapturing lost territory. Having observed Hannibal in action for over a decade, they had learned his strategies and, as a result, had become fiercer opponents. Though his army was dwindling in number—to less than forty thousand soldiers by 203 B.C.—Hannibal refused to surrender or be completely defeated.

Finally, when his brother Hasdrubal was killed, Hannibal realized the end was at hand. Along with twenty-four thousand soldiers, the warrior was recalled to Carthage in 203 B.C., but not before he had nearly defeated the Roman Republic, killing more than three hundred thousand Romans. In the meantime, Roman general Publius Scipio, the son of Hannibal's old opponent, crossed from Spain into Africa and was marching toward Carthage. Scipio defeated Hannibal and the army of Carthage in 202 B.C. at the battle of Zama.

Aftermath

The Second Punic War officially ended in 201 B.C., when Hannibal signed a peace treaty and agreed that he would never again attack Rome. Both Rome and Carthage were economically weakened by the seventeen-year-long ordeal. In fact, Rome's soaring inflation did not go down for fifteen years. Carthage recovered much more quickly, due in large part to Hannibal's leadership. After the war he served as head of state, repaying Rome its dues but also managing to reestablish Carthage as one of the Mediterranean's wealthiest city-states.

Exile. Though successful as a general and statesman, Hannibal was not fully appreciated by his government and was exiled in 195 B.C. Critics suggest that he probably never intended to keep peace with Rome; in 191 B.C. he joined Syrian leader Antiochus's attack on the city. For the next eight years, Hannibal joined various enemies of Rome in battle, but in 183 B.C., at the age of sixty-four, he was finally cornered. When the Romans demanded his surrender, he committed suicide by drinking poison. Before he died, he was quoted as saying: "Let us now put an end to the great anxiety of the Romans, who have thought it too lengthy, and too heavy a task, to wait for the death of a hated old man" (de Beer, p. 300).

Turning point. The Second Punic War proved to be a great turning point in history. Rome did not come so close to defeat for another six hundred years. Unchallenged after Hannibal's death, the Roman Republic grew by leaps and bounds and became one of the leading world powers by 46 B.C. Carthage, meanwhile, was incorporated into the Roman Republic after 146 B.C. and finally destroyed in A.D. 698 by the Arabs.

For More Information

de Beer, Sir Gavin. *Hannibal: Challenging Rome's Supremacy.* New York: Viking Press, 1969.

Lazenby, J. F. *Hannibal's War.* Warminster, England: Aris & Phillips, 1978.

Proctor, Dennis. *Hannibal's March in History.* New York: Clarendon Press, 1971.

Kao Tsu

c. 256-195 B.C.

Personal Background

Peasant beginnings. Kao Tsu (also spelled Gaozu), who was known as Liu Pang (or Liu Bang), was born in Pei, central China, around 256 B.C. He was raised in a humble home and received little or no education. Though he later became a low-ranking government official, it appears he had a long-standing distrust of the Ch'in (or Qin) dynasty (or ruling family).

Rebel. When Kao Tsu was a young man, several rebel groups were trying to overthrow the Ch'in dynasty. The Ch'in government had become very unpopular because of its rigid enforcement of the law and oppressive methods of governing. In 221 B.C. they consolidated power in China, defeating six rivals and solely ruling the vast territory with an iron fist. People were killed for speaking against the government, farmland was confiscated and citizens were enslaved for nonpayment of taxes, and most books were banned because Ch'in Emperor Shih Huang Ti considered too much knowledge a dangerous thing.

Local uprisings began occurring after the emperor's death in 210 B.C., and the threat of civil war loomed heavily throughout the land. Kao Tsu became directly involved in the conflict when he freed a group of prisoners under his guard and killed a local magistrate. Proclaiming himself the "Lord of Pei," he organized the pris-

▲ **A Han stone relief of a carriage on a low wooden beam bridge.**

Event: Beginning the Han dynasty.

Role: In 202 B.C. Kao Tsu led the successful overthrow of the Ch'in (Qin) dynasty and became the founder and first emperor of the Han dynasty. One of China's most culturally prominent periods, the Han dynasty produced great achievements in the arts, education, and sciences and made China as powerful as the Roman Empire.

oners and other rebellious locals into a small army and began attacking Ch'in forces throughout central China (Twitchett, p. 113).

In the fall of 209 B.C. Kao Tsu's soldiers joined forces with those of Hsiang Liang (also spelled Xiang Liang) and Hsiang Yu (or Xiang Yu), who had just assassinated the governor of K'uai-chi (or Kuaiji). The combination of soldiers making up the rebel army numbered in the thousands and posed a considerable threat to the Ch'in military. Less than a year later, the rebels captured the kingdom of Chu and established P'eng-ch'eng as their capital city. From there they began expanding throughout China, attempting to destroy the entire Ch'in empire.

Participation: Beginning the Han Dynasty

Victory over the Ch'in. In August 207 B.C. Kao Tsu captured Kuan-chung (also spelled Guanzhong), a key Ch'in stronghold. The following year he gained control of Lan-t'ien and won the entire region that had been the center of power of the Ch'in dynasty. Facing certain destruction, the Ch'in king surrendered, and Kao Tsu's forces took over the capital city of Hsien-yang (or Xianyang). Kao Tsu became the leader in place of the deposed king.

Though inexperienced, Kao Tsu proved to be a skillful and popular leader. He promptly took steps to abolish the strict laws of the Ch'in dynasty and institute a simple code of conduct and punishment. But before he could put many changes into practice, his power was challenged by a fellow general.

Internal battle. Despite the fact that Kao Tsu had captured the Ch'in capital and was becoming a popular leader, he faced some strong opposition to his rule. Hsiang Yu, an able and prominent military figure who had been Kao Tsu's ally a few years earlier in the battle for Chu, took control of the capital city and rebel forces. Hsiang Yu soon held the entire region. Once in charge, he divided all captured Ch'in territory into eighteen kingdoms and assigned them to various generals. Kao Tsu was given the territory of Han-chung (or Hanzhong), a remote region across the Ch'ing-ling (or Qingling) Mountains. A clear insult to the general who had engineered the capture of the Ch'in capital, the assignment angered Kao Tsu and led him to retaliate against Hsiang Yu.

Kao Tsu quickly recaptured the larger and more prominent Kuan-chung region, taking it from the kings Hsiang Yu had stationed there. He established a positive relationship with the local citizens, reorganized the territory, and began making policy changes. Kao Tsu gave the residents free use of farmland, parks, and lakes that once belonged to the Ch'in elite and banned taxes for two years; destroyed Ch'in temples and built altars to worship the god "Han"; and recruited new soldiers into his army to help expand his power. The army destroyed the last of the Ch'in dynasty in 206 B.C. and four years later completely defeated Kao Tsu's former ally turned enemy, Hsiang Yu.

Han dynasty begins. The Han dynasty began in 202 B.C., when Kao Tsu took control of China. (At this point, he officially changed his name from Liu Pang,

The People of Han

Though not his choice of kingdoms, the territory of Han-chung produced Kao Tsu's lasting nickname, "the king of Han." It is from this area and title that the Han dynasty also got its name.

his birth name, to Kao Tsu, the name of a Han temple, and adopted the title of emperor: *huang-ti* [or *huang-di*].) Emperor Kao Tsu was popular from the start of his reign. He immediately declared a national "amnesty" that returned farmland taken by the Ch'in government, freed citizens who had been sold into slavery, and offered tax exemptions to the neediest families. Kao Tsu also established his own family as the ruling family of China, from whose bloodline all succeeding emperors and empresses were to come.

Central government. Though in many respects Kao Tsu brought about great change in China, he did not completely abandon the Ch'in form of government. It remained centralized, with ultimate power vested in the emperor, although Kao Tsu did appoint three senior *san kung* (*sangong*), or statesmen, who advised him, and granted limited power to *chun-tzus* (*zhunzis*), or officials, who ran various government departments.

Kao Tsu divided China into fourteen provinces called commanderies and ten kingdoms. Governors and kings were given

▲ An 1887 engraving of a Chinese school. A renewed interest in education, science, literature, and the arts began to emerge under Kao Tsu's reign.

control of these regions (except the fourteenth commandery, which included the capital city of Changan and remained under Kao Tsu's direct control) but were granted little individual power. All appointments, funding, and major policy decisions were made by the emperor alone.

The Han family. In an effort to ward off attack from either the previous dynasty or neighboring civilizations, Kao Tsu sought to firmly unite his empire and make it a "family." He wrote:

> Now I, by the spiritual power of heaven, and by my capable gentlemen and high officials, have subjugated ... the Empire and made it into one family. I wish it to be enduring so that generation after generation should worship at my ancestral temple.... If there are any capable gentlemen or sirs who are willing to follow me and be friends with me, I can make them honourable and illustrious. (Kao Tsu in Capon, p. 65)

In addition to generously rewarding his officials, Kao Tsu drew people from all regions of China into his government and gained widespread loyalty. A writer in the first century A.D. claimed that Kao Tsu was "kindly disposed to others, benevolent and liked people." The writer further indicated that despite Kao Tsu's lack of education, "his mind was vast" (Capon, p. 61).

Han culture develops. China prospered under Kao Tsu's reign. Merchants, traders, and businessmen rose in social standing and became important members of society. A renewed interest in education, science, literature, and the arts began to emerge. Glazed pottery, large stone carvings, poetry, and histories of China were produced during this period, and a central university was established in Changan.

Aftermath

Emperor Kao Tsu's reign lasted until his death in 195 B.C. He was succeeded by his son, Hui-ti (or Huidi), who ruled until his early death in 188 B.C. Kao Tsu's wife, Empress Dowager Kao-gou, then ruled for the next nine years. Close members of the family succeeded her, serving successively through 9 B.C.

The Han dynasty provided a stable, centralized government in China. Though corruption and periodic rebellions existed, the four-hundred-year period was an exemplary and highly influential time in China's long history. Around 100 B.C., well after Kao Tsu's reign, Han China expanded into present-day Tibet, North Korea, and northern Vietnam, becoming a major world power that rivaled the Roman Empire. In A.D. 220 the dynasty finally came to an end, having been destroyed by internal disputes among government officials. War erupted and a stable government did not reemerge in China for another four hundred years.

The Idea of "Civil Service"

Han dynasty officials were civil service workers. In contrast to those in the Ch'in dynasty, who were all members of the aristocracy, Kao Tsu's officials were chosen by exam. Any male citizen could study, pass an exam, and become a civil servant of the Han dynasty. Once hired, the officials were rapidly promoted and earned a high degree of respect in society. This was a major break from the past and led to the value of education over birthright in China.

Capon, Edmund. *Princes of Jade*. London: Thomas Nelson & Sons, 1973.

McKay, John P., Bennett D. Hill, and John Buckler. *A History of World Societies*. Volume 1: *To 1715*. Boston: Houghton Mifflin, 1984.

Twitchett, Denis, and Michael Lowe, editors. *Cambridge History of China*. Volume 1. Cambridge, England: Cambridge University Press, 1986.

Bibliography

Brackman, Arnold C. *The Luck of Nineveh*. New York: McGraw-Hill, 1978.

Braidwood, R. *The Near East and the Foundations of Civilization*. Portland: University of Oregon Press, 1952.

Buxton, L. H. D. *China: The Land and the People*. New York: Oxford, 1929.

Bynner, W., and Kung Kang-hee. *The Jade Mountain*. New York: Knopf, 1929.

Cambridge History of Iran. Cambridge, England: Cambridge University Press, 1968.

Cary, M., and others. *The Oxford Classical Dictionary*. New York: Clarendon Press, 1949.

Chambers, Mortimer, and others. *The Western Experience*. 5th edition. New York: McGraw-Hill, 1991.

Cotterell, Arthur. *China: A Cultural History*. New York: Meridian, 1988.

Daniel, Glyn E. *A Hundred Years of Archeology*. London: Oxford University Press, 1950.

de Bary, William Theodore, Wing-tsit Chan, and Burton Watson. *Sources of Chinese Tradition*. New York: Columbia University Press, 1961.

Ellis, Edward S., and Charles F. Horne. *The World's Famous Events*. New York: Francis R. Niglutsch, 1914.

Epic of Gilgamesh. Translated by Maureen G. Kovacs. Stanford, California: Stanford University Press, 1989.

Fung, Yu-lan. *A Short History of Chinese Philosophy*. 2 vols. Princeton, New Jersey: Princeton University Press, 1952-53.

Garraty, John A., and Peter Gay, editors. *The Columbia History of the World*. New York: Columbia University Press, 1990.

Gernet, Jacques. *A History of Chinese Civilization*. Cambridge, England: Cambridge University Press, 1982.

Grant, Michael. *The History of Ancient Israel*. New York: Scribner's, 1984.

Gurney, O. R. *The Hittites*. New York: Viking, 1991.

Haywood, R. M. *Ancient Greece and the Near East*. New York: David McKay Co., 1964.

A History of the World in Story, Song, and Art. Boston: Houghton Mifflin, 1914.

Huang, Kerson, and Rosemary Huang. *I Ching*. New York: Workman, 1987.

Kaltenmark, Max. *Lao Tzu and Taoism*. Stanford, California: Stanford University Press, 1969.

BIBLIOGRAPHY

Kirk, G. S., and others. *The Presocratic Philosophers*. 2nd edition. Cambridge, England: Cambridge University Press, 1984.

Landay, Jerry M. *The House of David*. New York: Saturday Review/Dutton, 1973.

Lao Tzu. *Lao Tzu's Tao and Wu Wei*. Translated by Bhikshu Wai-Tao and Dwight Goodard. Santa Barbara, California: Dwight Goodard, 1935.

Latourette, Kenneth Scott. *A Short History of the Far East*. New York: Macmillan, 1964.

Levenson, J. R., and F. Schurmann. *China: An Interpretative History from the Beginnings to the Fall of Han*. Berkeley: University of California Press, 1971.

Lin Yutang, editor. *The Wisdom of Lao-tse*. New York: Modern Library, 1976.

Li Tao-ch'in. *The Book of Balance and Harmony*. San Francisco: North Point, 1989.

Lord, John. *Beacon Lights of History*. New York: Fords, Howard, and Hulbert, 1883.

McKay, John P., Bennett D. Hill, and John Buckler. *A History of World Societies*. Boston: Houghton Mifflin, 1984.

Mills, Dorothy. *The People of Ancient Israel*. New York: Scribner's, 1932.

Moran, William L. *The Amarna Letters*. Baltimore, Maryland: Johns Hopkins University Press, 1992.

Myers, Philip Van Ness. *Ancient History*. New York: Ginn, 1904.

Oates, Joan C. *Babylon*. London: Thames and Hudson, 1979.

Roman, Colin A. *The Shorter Science and Civilization in China*. 3 vols. Cambridge, England: Cambridge University Press, 1988.

Roux, George. *Ancient Iraq*. Cleveland, Ohio: World Publishing, 1962.

Schafer, Edward H. *The Golden Peaches of Samarkand*. Berkeley: University of California Press, 1963.

Seeger, Elizabeth. *The Pageant of Chinese History*. New York: David McKay Co., 1964.

Seeger, Elizabeth. *Eastern Religions*. New York: Crowell, 1973.

Sykes, Percy. *History of Persia*. New York: Columbia University Press, 1976.

Wallbank, T. Walter, Alastair M. Taylor, and Nels M. Bailkey. *Civilization: Past and Present*. 5th edition. Chicago: Scott, Foresman, 1965.

Index

Bold indicates entries and their page numbers; (ill.) indicates illustrations.

PROFILES IN WORLD HISTORY

Significant Events and the People Who Shaped Them
